TRANSYLVANIA
AND THE THEORY OF
DACO-ROMAN-RUMANIAN
CONTINUITY

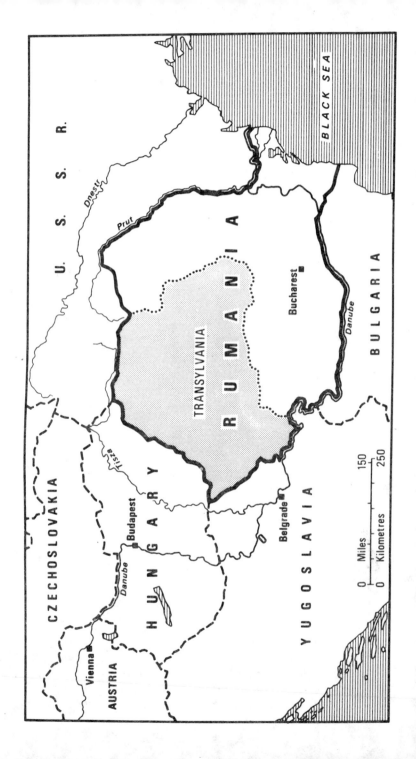

TRANSYLVANIA

AND THE THEORY OF DACO-ROMAN-RUMANIAN CONTINUITY

BOARD OF EDITORS

Stephen Borsody, Nandor Dreisziger
Adam Makkai, George Schöpflin

EDITOR
Louis L. Lőte

13-370

Published by the
COMMITTEE OF TRANSYLVANIA, INC.
1980

**REPRINT BY HUNYADI M M K
HAMILTON, ONTARIO
1991**

*Transylvania and the theory of
Daco-Roman-Rumanian continuity*

Copyrights © 1980 by Committee of Transylvania, Inc.
P. O. Box 3869, Rochester, New York 14610, U.S.A.

This is a special issue of the
CARPATHIAN OBSERVER
Volume 8, Number 1.

Library of Congress Catalog Card Number: 80-81573

Printed by Classic Printing Corporation, Cleveland, Ohio

CONTENTS

Map of the Danube Region 2

Introduction 6

The Daco-Rumanian Theory of Continuity:
Origins of the Rumanian Nation and Language.
    André DuNay 9

The Nationalities of Dacia during the Roman Period
    László Réthy 32

Who were the people living in the Carpathian Basin before
the Hungarian Conquest?
A Round-table discussion by
    György Györffy, Péter Hanák, László Makkai, András Mócsy
    Translated from Hungarian by
    Thomas Szendrey 42

La version la plus récente de la théorie de la continuité
Daco-Roumaine.
    Jean Csonka 55
The most recent version of the theory of Daco-Rumanian continuity
    Jean Csonka 71

Die albanisch-rumänische Wanderungsbewegung
(11.-13. Jahrhundert)
    Georg Stadtmüller 74
The Albanian-Rumanian Migrations (11th-13th centuries)
    Georg Stadtmüller 84

A Hungarian-Rumanian Dialogue: "At the Danube."
    The New Hungarian Quarterly (Winter 1978) 86

Ethnocide in Rumania
    Michael Sozan 93

Our Contributors 111

About the Editors 112

INTRODUCTION

This special issue of the *Carpathian Observer* is being published on the curious occasion of the 2050th anniversary of a rather obscure event in the ancient history of Dacia wnich is celebrated by modern Rumanians as the beginning of their national history in Transylvania. Under such bizarre circumstances our publication on the Transylvanian problem cannot but be controversial. Yet in compiling the historical material on Transylvania, our aim was to scrupulously observe the rules of fairness and honesty in scholarship.

Our publication deals with one of the most complex national conflicts of contemporary Europe. Victims of this conflicts are the Transylvanian Hungarians — over two million of them — living under Rumanian domination. They are known as minority Hungarians, not unlike their fellow Hungarians living in Czechoslovakia, Yugoslavia, and the Soviet Union.

The total number of these so-called minority Hungarians is close to four million, one fourth of all Hungarians living in the Danube region. They became minority Hungarians as a result of the territorial settlements following two World Wars. Most of them are living in areas where they are, or had been until recently, the majority. Now all of them are minorities in relationship to the total populations of the countries to which they were transferred by the peace treaties which unabashedly favored Hungary's rivals. Their fate is of paramount interest to all Hungarians wherever they may live.

The most burning issue among the Hungarian minority problems is that of the Transylvanian Hungarians under Rumanian rule, partly because they are the largest among the Hungarian minorities, partly because their treatment by the majority is the worst.

The historical background of the problem is concisely summed up in a recently published book, "Witnesses to Cultural Genocide", as follows:

Whereas the territory of Old Rumania, the Regat, has a largely ethnic Rumanian population, Transylvania has, and has had for centuries, an ethnically mixed population. After the Hungarians entered the Danube basin after the Ninth Century and founded the Kingdom of Hungary in 1000, they attached Transylvania to the Kingdom and settled it. From then on, Transylvania remained part of the Kingdom—the Crownlands of St. Stephen—even during the 150 years of Ottoman occupation, when the Kingdom of Hungary was divided into three. Transylvania was at times an autonomous principality, and signed the Treaty of Westphalia, which ended the Thirty Years War, in that capacity in 1648; nevertheless its princes emphasized the role of the province as guaranteeing the legal continuity of the Hungarian state. When Transylvania became part of Rumania after the First World War in 1918-1920, the annexation of Transylvania represented the fulfillment of a powerful Rumanian nationalist aspiration. It was beyond doubt that Transylvania had a majority Rumanian population but it was also the homeland of substantial Hungarian and German minorities. These groups found that in satisfying Rumanian national aspirations their own suffered. The newly enlarged Rumanian state regarded the Hungarian minority as a potential or actual threat to its security and introduced a variety of discriminatory measures against it. Underlying this move was a fear that just as Rumania had obtained Transylvania on the basis of its Rumanian population, so the Hungarians might do the same on the basis of its Hungarian population. These fears were realized in 1940 when the northern two-fifths of Transylvania was temporarily reattached to Hungary.

After the war there were hopes that the new communist regime would pursue a more equitable policy toward the Hungarians, but these hopes were soon confounded.

Our aim in preparing this publication is to make widely available several scholarly analyses of the Transylvanian problem. We regret that nationalist propaganda obscures and distorts this problem, so vital as it is to so many people. Our interest in the problem of Hungarians in Rumania is not motivated by Hungarian considerations alone. The Transylvanian problem, apart from being a local conflict, has broader significance as well. Since it engenders jealousy and bitter hostility, it is a major stumbling block to international harmony in that part of Europe in general. We are hopeful that our effort will promote not merely the understanding of the Transylvanian problem but also advance the cause of reconciliation everywhere in the Danube region.

Peace in the Danube region is being undermined by relentless national conflict and reckless propaganda which distorts both the past and present. Yet it is our conviction that truth can prevail over falsehood, reason over emotions, reality over myth. In that spirit we look forward to the day when Rumanians and Hungarians will join hands and work together for peace for their own good and for the good of all peoples of the Danube region tormented for so long by national hostility.

The Editors

THE DACO-RUMANIAN THEORY OF CONTINUITY:
ORIGINS OF THE
RUMANIAN NATION AND LANGUAGE

By
ANDRÉ DU NAY

Rumania will celebrate this year the 2050th anniversary of "the creation of the first centralized and independent Dacian state." They will claim that the Dacians were the ancestors of the Rumanian people and this will be propagated also in several Western countries. Behind this claim, there is the theory of Roman continuity in Dacia Traiana. It is now official ideology in Rumania, and no criticism of it is allowed. It is therefore necessary to investigate the circumstances behind this peculiar celebration and to provide an objective analysis of its significance and the theory behind it.

1. The Appearance of the Theory of Continuity

The historical background.

As shown by historical records[1], acheological finds[2], and ancient Hungarian place-names[3], most of Transylvania was populated by Hungarians during the 10th-12 centuries. Until the mid-16th century, it was part of Hungary. During the 12th and the 13th centuries, Saxons (Germans) were settled in certain areas, especially in the south. After the occupation of large parts of Hungary by the expanding Turkish empire in the mid-16th century, Transylvania became independent and continued, for centuries to come, the traditions of Hungary. Towards the end of the 17th century, the Turks were driven out of Hungary and Transylvania was subjugated by the Habsburg empire.

The first documentary mentioning Rumanians in Transylvania refers to the year 1210 AD (cf. B. Jancsó: *Erdély tör-*

ténete (The History of Transylvania/, Cluj-Kolozsvár, 1931, p. 42). Their number was, however, in the first centuries after their appearance, very low. This is apparent from the analysis of placenames. An investigation of the names of villages existing today gives the following picture: Before the end of the 13th century, the names of 511 villages in Transylvania and in the Banat appear in documents, of which only three are of Rumanian origin. Up to 1400 AD, 1757 villages are mentioned, out of which 76 (4.3%) have names of Rumanian origin (cf. Kniezsa, 1943, p. 158). In the following centuries the number of Rumanians continued to increase: in the 1700s AD, they amounted to about 40% of the total population. During the 18th century, the number of Rumanians in Transylvania increased even more. The cause of this was mainly the immigration of peasants from Muntenia and Moldavia, the Rumanian countries, where they lived in squalor, being exploited by the Turks as well as by their own lords.

Although quite a few Transylvanian Rumanians were granted nobility by the Habsburgs during the 18th century, most of the Rumanians remained bondsmen and shepherds. Meanwhile, the ideas of the Reformation and Enlightenment have found vigorous resonance among the Hungarians and Saxons of Transylvania. In the spirit of these ideas, many of them considered that it was their duty to further the cultural advancement of the Rumanians. It was in Transylvania that the Rumanian language was first introduced as the lithurgical language of the Byzantine Rite Catholic Church, replacing Slavonic, which the common people did not understand. The first books in the Rumanian language were printed in Transylvania, on the initiative of Saxon and Hungarian noblemen and priests, who also paid the costs of publishing. In these books printed in southern Transylvania, in the second half of the 16th century by Dean Coresi, "we find the beginnings of our literary language"—C. Giurescu states in *Istoria romãnilor,* (Bucharest, 1975, p. 387). Almost a century had to pass until the first book in Rumanian was printed in Muntenia (in 1640; cf. *Istoria Romãniei in date,* ed. C. Giurescu, 1971, p. 136). After the Union of the Byzantine Rite Catholic Church with Rome (in 1700), the number of Rumanian schools increased and Rumanian youths were in increasing numbers sent to foreign universities. Thus, a class of Rumanian intellectuals developed in Transylvania in an epoch in which this would not have been possible in the Rumanian countries of Muntenia and Moldavia. Ironically, it was this intelligentsia, whose existence would not have been possible without the help of the other nationalities of Transylvania (the Hungarians and the Saxons), which started the struggle for political rights of the Rumanians. One of the first and most important protagonists of these intellectuals was bishop Innocentius Klein, who forwarded a series of demands to the provincial government of Transylvania and to the Habsburg court in Vienna. In these, he asked for the recognition of the Rumanians as the fourth nation in Transylvania. One of his arguments was that the Rumanians outnumber any other single nation in the country, but more significantly he claimed that the Rumanians originated from emperor Trajan's colonists and have been living in the country ever since the Roman conquest. *This is the first formulation of the theory of Roman continuity in Dacia Traiana. It was to support a distinctly Rumanian political struggle in the first half of the 18th century.*

The most important petition in this struggle was the *Supplex Libellus Valachorum*, forwarded to king Leopold the 2nd in 1791. Its authors are not exactly known but it is considered as the collective work of the leading Rumanian intellectuals of that time: S. Micu-Klein, I. Molnar-Piuariu, I. Budai-Deleanu, I. Mehes. P. Maior, Ch. Sincai and others. The main points were the following:

> The Rumanians should receive all the civil rights the other nations posses: Rumanians should be admitted to the provincial Assembly and should be permitted to hold official positions in proportion to their number; they should receive the right to call together a national assembly which could elect delegates who would represent them wherever this would be needed; Rumanian place-names should be used in all areas in which Rumanians are living; communities with a Rumanian majority should use the Rumanian name while in those in which the Rumanians are in the minority, bilingual Hungarian-Rumanian or Saxon-Rumanian names should be used. (Indidentally in the text of the petition, the word 'Vlach' is used instead of 'Rumanian'.)

The 'Libellus' claimed, as did earlier demands of this kind, that the Rumanians were first in Transylvania:

"The Rumanian nation is by far the most ancient of all nations of our epoch, since it is certain and proved by historical evidence, by a never interrupted tradition, by the similarity of the language, traditions and customs, that it originates from the Roman colonists brought here at the beginning of the 2nd century A.D. by emperor Trajan . . ."

The 'Transylvanian School' (Şcoala ardeleană).

The ideas of the Enlightenment, the discovery of Latin as the ancestor of the Rumanian language and, above all, the political struggle for the rights of the Rumanians, inspired a new movement in Transylvania in the second half of the 18th century. This movement was called *Şcoala ardeleană* (Transylvanian School). One of the first and most important works produced was *Elementa linguae daco-romanae sive valachicae,* the first grammar of the Rumanian language. Written by Gh. Sincai and S. Micu-Klein, it was published in Vienna in 1780.

The message of the Transylvanian School may be summarized briefly as follows: The Latin origin of the Rumanian language; the unity of this language spoken in Muntenia, Moldavia and parts of Transylvania; the theory of continuity, i.e., the idea that the Rumanian language developed in the same territory where the Roman colony of Dacia Traiana was situated.

Out of these three ideas, only the first two correspond to reality. In detail, however, many errors were propagated even with these. Thus, for instance, Sincai and Micu-Klein assumed that Rumanian derived from classical Latin. But it was P. Maior in particular who defended the idea that the Latin language spoken by the common people must have given rise to the neo-Latin languages, so also to the Rumanian.

The aims of this vigorous intellectual movement were not primarily scientific. The study of Rumanian history and language was developed, in the first place, to be used in the struggle of Rumanian intellectuals for more political rights for their own people. This is also stated in several modern publications about the epoch in question.

Ideas about the glorious past and great importance to all mankind of one's own nation, and, in general, the ideology of romantic nationalism, were widespread in Europe in this age. Thus, several circumstances, internal as well as external, contributed to the development and to the strength of this Rumanian movement in Transylvania.

Petru Maior:

The history of the origin of the Rumanians in Dacia.

One of the most important works produced by the Transylvanian School is *Istoria pentru începutul romînilor în Dachia* (The History of the origin of the Rumanians in Dacia) by P. Maior, published in Buda, the Hungarian capital, in 1812. The author was in that epoch a licenser of the press at the printing office in Buda.

The author's aim with this book was to provide arguments in the struggle for the rights of Rumanians living in Transylvania and to repudiate those authors who did not agree with the idea that the Rumanians originate from the soldiers and colonists of Trajan.

Maior's chief ideas concerning the origin of the Rumanians may be summarized as follows:

The Rumanians are descendents of those Roman colonists who were brought to Dacia by emperor Trajan after the conquest in 106 AD. The Dacians were either exterminated in the war with the Romans or fled the country; the Rumanians are thus of purely Roman origin, a "pure race".—In 274 AD, when the Roman empire left Dacia Traiana, most of the population remained in the country and continued living there ever since those times, mainly as sedentary peasants.

Although many of these ideas have been refuted by later Rumanian scholars, this work and, in general, the entire ideology of the Transylvanian School did not only have strong influence upon Rumanian historical thinking but *still affects writing of history in Rumania today.*

Maior uses arguments of "historical logic", confuses assumptions with facts and uses, not infrequently, extremely implausible hypotheses and wrong data, if they fit his reasoning. He does not refrain from attacking the person of the author whose ideas he does not like.

13

2. The Theory of Continuity Refuted:
O. Densusianu and Al. Philippide

Two events in the 19th century were of decisive importance in Rumanian history: the fact that Muntenia and Moldavia gained independence and were subsequently united in 1859. This was an epoch of national awakening and of the development of a national intelligentsia. A problem of crucial importance was, evidently, the aim of creating a literary language; the establishment of a uniform grammar and orthography; what methods to follow in adopting new lexical elements, etc.

The Latin character of Rumanian had been generally accepted long ago and, almost generally, also the theory that it developed from Latin spoken in Dacia Traiana. There were, however, Rumanian scholars who were sceptical and sought alternative explanations, as for example Filaret Scriban, who asserted that the Rumanians were of Sarmatian origin. In general, however, Rumanian origins were not studied too intensely in that era. Nevertheless, in due course, knowledge about the Rumanian language increased. During the last decades of the 19th century, Rumanian linguistics established itself as an independent discipline and professional linguists appeared who occupied themselves with problems of linguistics alone. Thus, the pre-requisites for a new synthesis were created, for a fresh look upon a problem hitherto not studied by modern scientific methods: the question of the origin of the Rumanian language.

Ovid Densusianu (1873-1938), the disciple of Gaston Paris and Adolf Tobler, was a linguist in whom extensive knowledge of the Rumanian language, his mother-tongue, was coupled with a sincere, almost passionate desire for finding the truth. His chief work, *Histoire de la langue roumaine* (*I: Les origines*; *II: Le seizieme siècle*) appeared in 1901.

Densusianu collected and weighed a vast amount of linguistic material which gave him a solid basis for the drawing of conclusions. He also recognized the key role the shepherd way of life of the Rumanians played in the history of their language. All the facts point to a territory in close contact with Italy not only until the 3rd century AD but very much later. At the same time, no linguistic phenomena indicate any contact with the populations which are known to have been living north of the lower Danube in the centuries after the abandonment of Dacia Traiana by the Romans. Densusianu concludes that the area in which Rumanian was formed must have been Illyria.

It is easy to imagine that, as I. Iordan put it, this book was "a revelation" (I. Iordan, *Lingvistica*, 1975, p. 98, note 11). Finally, 90 years after P. Maior's *History of the origins of the Rumanians in Dacia,* every Rumanian had the opportunity to read a scientific treatise about the origin of his mother-tongue written by an objective and well-prepared Romance scholar.

Fully aware of the importance of his findings and conclusions, Densusianu addresses future Rumanian philologists, trying to persuade them to break with tradition that impedes the progress of Rumanian philology:

> "Patriotism as it is conceived today in Rumania will impede the progress of Rumanian philology for a long time to come, hindering the investigators from seeking and telling the truth. The true patriot is not he who seeks to denature the facts and to deceive himself, and the scientist forgets his duty if he does not tell the truth no matter how painful it may be." (O. Densusianu: *Histoire de la langue roumaine,* 1901; in the 1975 edition, p. 26).

Densusianu was not alone in Rumania in conducting impartial research with the passionate interest to find the truth about the origins of his mother-tongue. This scholar in Bucharest had a colleague in Iasi, the capital of Moldavia, who also wrote a large treatise about the problem: Alexandru Philippide (1859-1934).

3. The Theory of Continuity Today
The changed political situation.

In 1920, the struggle fought by the Rumanians of Transylvania for their national rights came to a resoundingly successful end: the peace treaty after the First World War transferred entire Transylvania, including its purely Hungarian and Saxon areas, to Rumania. The roles have changed. Now the Rumanians became the ruling element and the Hungarians had to struggle for their rights as citizens of the Rumanian nation-state, together with the Saxons and other minor ethnic groups.

Between the two World Wars, much work was done in order to prove the continuity of the Romans (and Rumanians) from the 4th through the 11th centuries, especially by archeological investigations in Transylvania. Constantin Daicoviciu expressed repeatedly his conviction that definitive archeological proofs have been found; for example in his preface to D. Protase's *Problema continuităţii în Dacia în lumina arheologiei şi numismaticii* (The Problem of the continuity in Dacia in the light of archeology and numismatics). It should be pointed out, however, that opposite views were not suppressed: *Originea rominilor* by Al. Philippide appeared at that time and even a Hungarian book in which the history of the Rumanians is presented entirely according to the "immigrationist" view could appear in 1931 in Cluj-Kolozsvár; See B. Jancsó: *Erdély története* (The History of Transylvania), ed. Minerva.

Such opinions are entirely absent from the writings published in Rumania during the past three decades. Today, every text dealing with this problem, from newspaper articles to scientific treatises, defends unanimously the theory of continuity. The theory is not presented and treated as one of several possibilities, seriously questioned by several Rumanian and foreign scholars, but rather as an axiom.

A single exception would be a new edition of O. Densusianu's *Histoire de la langue roumaine* in 1975, but this publication in French reached only a very limited number of readers. Moreover, it was provided with a preface and notes in which Densusianu's arguments and ideas are criticized and "corrected".

Thus, the main idea of continuity is retained. More disquieting is the fact that the attitude of earlier epochs, in which the adversaries of this "Rumanian thesis" were considered people of bad intentions and enemies of the Rumanians still prevails.

In the most recent textbook for university students about the history of the Rumanian language, any idea opposing the theory of continuity is declared both un-scientific and chauvinistic!

16

The heritage of P. Maior.

No historian accepts today such obvious errors of P. Maior as the assertion that the Cumans and the Petcheneges were Rumanians, that the Rumanian "race" is purely of Roman origin or the belief about the extermination of all the Dacians during the wars with the Roman empire.

However, several of Maior's arguments are still used, often in the same form as Maior presented them some 170 years ago. Thus, "logical" considerations, without any material evidence from written sources or any other date are still used extensively.

The main arguments in favor of the theory of continuity have been derived, for a long time, from archeological investigations. This is the case also today; the arguments forwarded within the areas of history and linguistics (including onomastics) are mainly defensive in nature.

A number of settlements and cemeteries from the 4th and 5th centuries, but also from later epochs, have been considered to have been left by a Romanized population. Roman coins found north of the lower Danube are said to demonstrate the existence there of "Daco-Romans". The same significance is claimed for a number of objects of Christian character dated to the 4th and 5th centuries. Thus, an *ex voto*, from the 4th century, found near Medgyes (German Mediasch, Rum. Medias) in Transylvania with the inscription "Ego Zenovius votum posui" (I, Zenovius, have placed this present) is said to be

"a very important proof of the old age of Christianity in the Latin language in Dacia and of the continuity of the Daco-Roman population after the retreat of the legions" (Giurescu: *Istoria românilor,* 1975, p. 148). (The actual list given includes villages like "Bicsad in the [country] of Oaş, county Satu Mare, Racsa, etc.)

Now it is a peculiar fact that not a single name of those villages and areas in which these putative "Daco-Romans" lived is of Rumanian origin: —oas derives from Hungarian *Avas* (*avas* 'scrubby, bushy'), Orasul Nou, earlier *Ioaras:* from Hung. *Új-város* (*Abaújváros*) ('New Town'), mentioned in a document from 1270 AD as *Nova Civitas* or *Wynarus* (— *Wywarus*) and in 1370 as *Wyuaras, Wyuaros.* (The modern Rumanian form is thus the translation of Hung. *Újváros.*)

Satu Mare, earlier *Sătmar*, from Hung. *Szatmár*, first mentioned in a document from 1213 as *castrum Zathmar* (the name originates from a German personal name). (The modern Rumanian name developed by popular etymology; it means 'Great Village'.)

Bicsad is borrowed from Hung. *Bikszád* or *Bükszád* (Hung. *bükk* 'beech', *szád* 'opening'), mentioned in a document from 1478 as *Bykzad*.

Racsa, Hung. *Ráksa*, is first mentioned in a document (from 1493) as *Rakos*, in another from 1512 as *Raksa*. (These data were taken from C. Suciu: *Dicţionar istoric al localitaţilor din Transilvania*, Bucharest, vol. I and II, 1967, 1968.)

As regards the value of these pictures in proving "the continuity of the 'Daco-Romans' in the Carpathian space", no comments are necessary, exactly as it is not necessary today to point out, for example, that Rumanian *birau* 'judge' does not derive, as P. Maior believed, from Latin *vir magnus* but from Hungarian *bíró* 'judge'.

A new interpretation:

The Dacians as "the most significant ethnic component of the Rumanian nation".

A new interpretation of recent years is the emphasis upon the Dacians as the great ancestors of the Rumanian people. The Transylvanian School, as we have seen above, defended an extremely Latinistic view. It considered only the Latin elements of Rumanian as really belonging to this language and denied all connections with the Dacians, who did not, according to this concept, survive the Roman conquest of their country.

Today the trend seems to be the opposite of this. It is now argued that the most important part of the ancestors of the Rumanians were the Dacians, autochthonous in the whole territory of present day Rumania.

Giurescu describes this relatively new concept as follows: In Dacia Traiana, Roman domination lasted for only about 170 years. In Pannonia and in Britannia, the Romans were in power twice as long and still, no lasting Roman population developed in these countries. Why? Giurescu asks.

18

"Because only with functionaries and people coming from other areas no new aspect, no new life may be imprinted in a territory" (Giurescu, 1975, p. 127).

Romaniazation was successful in Dacia, says Giurescu, because the Romans

". . . represented a superior civilization, a material and cultural creation which synthesized an entire evolution of hundreds of years and as such, it won over the autochthones. These, increasingly convinced and drawn by the advantages of Roman life, learned the language of the conquerors, took their names and were Romanized" (Giurescu, 1975, p. 127).

Romans, i.e., people from Italy, were very few in Dacia Traiana, states Giurescu rightly (pp. 95 and 125). The colonists in that province were mostly Thracian, Illyrian, Pannonian, people from the East and Greeks. But the number of all these together "did not exceed that of the autochthones, the Dacians" (p. 135). And this people "is on the basis of our nation as *the most significant ethnic component*" (p. 62; emphasis added).

The festivities in 1980 of "the creation of the first centralized and independent Dacian state" emphasize this new trend. One may ask whether the 2000th anniversary was celebrated in 1930? No anniversary of any kind was even mentioned then! This is no surprise, since the year 1980 as the 2050th anniversary of the first Dacian state was chosen quite arbitrarily. Neither the year in which king Burebista seized power, nor any period of time during which he united the Dacians is recorded. On the basis of a few, vague descriptions, one may guess that these events happen between 82 and 70, or even 60, BC. What then, is the reason for this remarkable celebration?

The West German publicist Viktor Meier gives, in the *Frankfurter Allgemeine Zeitung,* July 18, 1978, a concise answer:

"One wonders why exactly 2050 years and whether this is known with any precision. Professor Hadrian Daicoviciu of the University of Klausenburg, (German "Klausenburg"; Hungarian "Kolozsvár"; Rumanian "Cluj"), as the successor of his father the leader of Rumanian research on the Dacians, gives a plausible answer: The leadership asked the scientists for a date in the near future which would be suitable for an exhaustive presentation of the significance of the Dacians in Rumanian history."

4. Is There Any Evidence of Continuity?

The first known inhabitants of Transylvania, described by Herodotos, in the 6th-4th centuries BC, were the *Agathyrses,* probably an Iranian people. They left many material remains in Transylvania and also in Moldavia. In the third and second centuries BC, a considerably dense population of *Celts* were living in Transylvania and in the Banat. Settlements and cemeteries used by them were discovered, so far, at 140 places.[4] The Celts disappeared towards the end of the second century BC; they were replaced by the Dacians.

The Balkan peninsula south of the Danube was, during the last centuries BC, conquered by the Roman empire. North of the river, the Getae and the Dacians lived and seem to have prospered in that epoch. The development of the technology of iron and gold, as well as commercial contacts with Greek and Roman merchants strengthened their economy. In the first half of the 1st century BC, a king called Buerebista (also "Buruista" etc.) organized the Dacians and several other populations into a powerful empire.

In what year Burebista seized power is not known. In *Istoria României în date,* (ed. by C. Giurescu, 1971, p. 26), the year 70 BC is given without any further comment.

Towards the end of the 1st century AD, another strong ruler, Decebal, united the Dacian tribes again into a centralized empire. He fought the Romans with some success, but these defeated him finally and made him to pay tributes. In the first decade of the 2nd century AD, emperor Trajan waged wars with the Dacians with the aim to conquer their country and succeeded in 106 AD. Decebal committed suicide and his army was dispersed. The new Roman colony north of the lower Danube was called *Dacia Traiana*; it comprised what is now Oltenia, parts of the Banat and of Transylvania. It was dominated by the Roman empire until 275 AD, i.e., for about 170 years.

Outside the colony, several barbarian populations, Goths and other Old Germanic peoples, Sarmatians, free Dacians, Carps, etc., were living and conducted several incursions into the territory dominated by the Romans. Archeological finds show that these peoples settled in the area of the former colony after 275 AD.

In the following century, the Dacians disappear from the scene of history.

Much has been written about the question of the grade of Romanization of the Dacians within the colony of Dacia Traiana; we refer here only to A. Du Nay, 1977, chapters 3 and 4.

About the language of the Dacians.

Very little is preserved of this language. Since it is assumed that it was related to Thracian, one has tried to find similarities between Rumanian and Thracian, which is somewhat better known. Also the designation "Thraco-Dacian" has been used, although it is questionable whether this is really justified.

I. Russu has compiled a Rumanian-Thracian dictionary with almost 200 Thracian words (Russu, 1967, pp. 138-143). Among these, there are 11 words whose Rumanian counterpart is considered to derive from the substratum of Rumanian, (for example *copil* 'child', Thracian *-centus, -poris, tap* 'he-goat', Thracian *Buzo-, Cozeil-*; *spînz* 'hellebore', Thracian *prodiarna*; etc.). If this substratum were Thracian, one would expect some correspondence between these words. This is, however, not the case; there is not a single Rumanian word which reliably could be shown to originate from what is left to us from Thracian.

> "The fact that we do not possess ancient or medieval attestations of the autochthonous lexical elements is a grave gap in the documentary material which could throw light upon the problem of the beginnings and the ancient phase in the development of the Rumanian and Albanian idioms and popular communities" (Russu, 1967, p. 215).

Thus, although this could be caused by the chance, the number of preserved Thracian words being very low, it must be stated that there is no evidence to support the idea that Rumanian developed from Thracian. The same applies, of course, to Dacian.

After 275 AD.

It is reasonbale to assume that a part of the inhabitants of Dacia Traiana remained in the province after its abandonment by the Romans. This was the case in Noricum, Raetia, Britannia, not to mention the Balkan provinces. In the case of Dacia, no one has proved that these spoke Latin, but we may assume it. In all the above mentioned provinces, however, the Romans who remained in their places after the retreat of the Roman army and administration, were sooner or later assimilated to the conquering populations and disappeared latest after some centuries.

In post-Roman Dacia Traiana, clear-cut evidence (archeological remains) of Carps and free Dacians, Sarmatians, Goths, Gepidae, Huns and, somewhat later, Avars and Slavs were found. On the basis of the fact that many material remains show the influence of Roman style and customs, one has argued that these remains indicate a Roman population. This cannot be accepted, however, because earthernware of Roman provincial style, a few objects with Latin inscriptions, Roman coins and other similar finds are described not only from South East Europe but from almost every part of the European continent. Coins, for example, are very numerous not only north of the lower Danube but north of the entire course of this river as well as north of the river Rhein; earthernware of Roman style was not only used but also imitated in far away areas. The "Roman provincial" style was, in other words, widespread in Europe.

5. The Testimony of the Rumanian Language

As we have seen neither historical records nor archeological finds confirm the theory of continuity. These conclusions are, however, negative and we have to ask now *where*, then, did the Rumanian language develop and what was the nature of that language which, by Romanization, evolved into modern Rumanian?

Although many details remain to be clarified, the analysis of the Rumanian language gives decisive information regarding the principal questions. This has been discovered long ago by linguists; it is sufficient to mention here Gaston Paris and Ovid Densusianu. We can here, of course, only give the main points, a more detailed discussion is found in A. Du

Nay 1977. The question to be put is the following: Does the Rumanian language, as it is today, show vestiges which indicate that its speakers lived north of the lower Danube already beginning with the end of the 3rd century AD (when the Romans abandoned Dacia Traiana), in the vicinity of Old Germanic, Avarian and other migratory populations? This should be the case if the theory of continuity would be the true explanation of the present existence of the Rumanians north of the lower Danube. But this is not the case.

Instead, there are a large number of features in Rumanian which must have developed in a community living in the Roman empire several centuries *after* the abandonment of Dacia Traiana by the Romans and in the vicinity of populations very different from those which once lived north of the lower Danube.

The construction of the perfect with the help of the verb *habeo* developed in Late Latin, after the 4th century; e.g. *episcopum invitatum habes* "you have invited the bishop", Rumanian *ai invitat pe episcop*.

A number of new expressions and lexical elements were formed in Late Latin, as for example *Sclavus, Sclavinus* "Slav" Rumanian *schiau*; *primo vere* "spring" Rum. *primăvară* (cf. Italian *primavera*), *aeramen* (instead of classical Latin *aes*) "metal, copper; Rum, *arama* "copper" (cf. Italian *rame* "cooper").

Lexical elements shared by Rumanian and northern Italian dialects.

Already Gaston Paris pointed out the importance of these elements, which in many cases are exclusively found in Rumanian and certain Italian dialects. O. Densusianu gives a detailed description and concludes that these are vestiges from an epoch in which the ancestors of the Rumanians lived in close contacts with the population in northern Italy. We mention here only some of them:

From Latin *expanticare,* in Venetian and Milanese *spantegar,* in Rumanian *spînteca* "to rip up"; from Latin *implenire,* Friulian *impleni,* Rumanian *împlini* "to fill, to carry out"; Venetian *ol cel della bocha,* Rumanian *cerul gurei*

23

"palate", lit. "the sky of the mouth"; Latin *reus* "guilty", in the dialect of Campobasso *re* "bad", in Rumanian *răp* "bad", etc.

Vestiges in the Rumanian language of Late Latin features and words shared with northern Italian dialects indicate that the ancestors of the speakers of Rumanian lived, at least until the 7th century AD, in close contacts with the Latin-speaking populations of Italy. From the abandonment of Dacia Traiana in 275 AD, however, the Danubian *limes* was the frontier between the Roman empire and "Barbaricum". Controlled by the Roman army, it was a military border, with fortifications, whose chief function was defending the empire against invading armies from the north. Although not totally impermeable, this frontier did not permit everyday contacts between the population of the Roman empire in the south and those living north of the lower Danube. Consequently, the phonetical, morphological and lexicological changes of the 3rd-6th centuries AD in the Latin language could not have penetrated into the language of a population living north of the lower Danube. The domination for some period of time during the 4th century of a strip of territory along the lower Danube does not change this (cf., for more details, Du Nay, 1977, pp. 214-216).

The relation between Rumanian and Albanian.

To the pre-Latin elements of Rumanian belong about 120 words which may be divided into several well-defined semantic groups, as for example parts of the human body, terms of kinship, plants and animals and, most significantly, *shepherd words,* the largest group. These words were used by a population living close to nature, in the mountains, whose main occupation was the rising of animals (sheep). Expressions designating urban phenomena are absent from this group of words. The question is now, what population spoke the language from which these pre-Latin elements survived in Rumanian?

There are no historical records to give any indication in this respect. As we have seen, elements of Thracian, Dacian and other ancient languages preserved in Greek and Latin texts are of no help, since there is not a single reliable correspondence between these words and Rumanian ones. The

24

language once spoken somewhere in South East Europe from which Rumanian originates is simply not preserved in writing.

There is, however, another Balkan language, extant today, in which most (about 80%) of the above mentioned lexical elements do exist. This is one of the most ancient languages of the Balkan peninsula: Albanian. Such words are, for example: Rumanian *buză* Albanian *buzë* 'lip; rim, edge'; Rum. *baci* Alb. *bac* 'shepherd in charge of a sheepfold'; Rum. *gălbează, călbează* Alb. *gëlbazë, këlbazë* 'sheep pox; liverworst'; Rum. *vatră* Alb. *vater, vatra* 'hearth, fireplace; house, dwelling' and many others (cf. A. Du Nay, 1977, pp. 62-70; A. Rosetti, ed., *Istoria limbii române*, Edit. Acad. RSR, vol. II, 1969, pp. 327-356).

SEMANTIC GROUP	Number of words:	
	Also in Albanian	Not in Albanian
Man: parts of the human body, sex, age family relations	9	2
Plants and animals	22	5
Agriculture	2	1
Specific shepherd words	25	5
Cloths; human dwelling; tools; nature, geography; popular mythology; other nouns adverbs and verbs	42	9
Total	100	22

Table 1. Pre-Latin words in Rumanian. (After A. Du Nay: *The Early History of the Rumanian language*, 1977, p. 61, table 3.)

There also are similarities between the two languages concerning phonology and morphology. Thus, the definite article occurs at the end of the noun in both languages and, what is more remarkable:

"these two languages coincide in the use of this element of speech in the smallest details of its syntactical position, which contradicts the assumption of a spontaneous evolution in each of these two languages" (E. Çabej: "Unele probleme ale istoriei limbii albanese", in *Studii şi cercetari lingvistice*, X, 4, 1959, p. 531).

Out of a large number of similarities concerning phraseology and lexical elements, we mentione the following:

'It is proper, it is convenient' may be expressed by Rumanian *Ce cu cale* and Albanian *ishte me udhe* which literally mean 'it is with way'.

'That hurts me': Rum. *îmi vine rău*, Alb. *i erdhi keq* 'it comes me bad'.

'Uvula': Rum. *omuşor*, Alb. *njerith* 'Little man'.

To strengthen the sense of a noun, 'great thing' (Rum. *mare lucru*, Alb. *pun'e madhe*) may be added; etc.

The Latin elements of these languages also show similar features, as for instance parallel changes of meaning:

Latin *falx* 'sickle, scythe' — Rum. *falcă*, Alb. *felqine* 'jaw, cheek'.

Latin *draco* 'dragon' — Rum. *drac*, Alb. *dreq* 'devil'.

Latin *horreo* 'I fear, I am shocked' — Rum. *urăsc*, Alb. *urrej* 'I hate'.

Latin *veteranus* 'soldier who has served his time' — Rum. *bătrîn*, Alb. *vjetër* 'old', and many others.

Albanian and Rumanian are now, of course, different languages. This is explained by the difference in the degree of Romanization and by the different history of the two populations after their gradual separation not very long after the Roman influence. While the ancestors of the Rumanians were almost totally Romanized, those of the Albanians only borrowed a number of Latin elements but retained most of their own language.

The common elements as regards the ancient word stock, the similarities in the structure of the two languages and in the Latin elements indicate that the ancestors of the Rumanians and of the Albanians were the same, or very closely related. Thus, if we know the territory in which the ancient Albanians were living, we may also know the approximate areas of the ancient Rumanians.

According to G. Stadtmüller: *Forschungen zur albanischen Frühgeschichte* (1966; pp. 95-96, 120), the Mati district

26

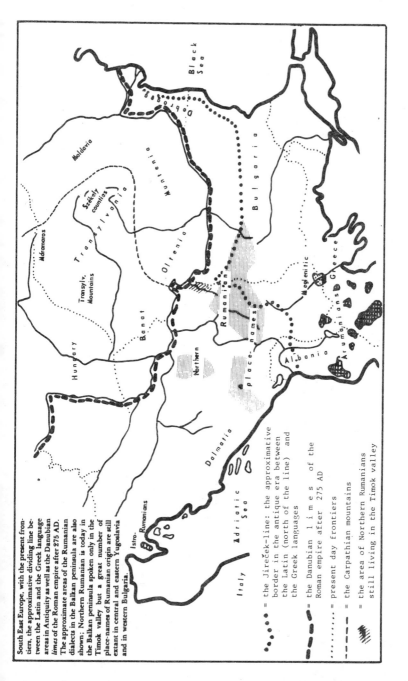

South East Europe, with the present frontiers, the approximative dividing line between the Latin and the Greek language areas in Antiquity as well as the Danubian *limes* of the Roman empire after 275 AD. The approximate areas of the Rumanian dialects in the Balkan peninsula are also shown: Northern Rumanian is today in the Balkan peninsula spoken only in the Timok valley but a great number of place-names of Rumanian origin are still extant in central and eastern Yugoslavia and in western Bulgaria.

●●●● = the Jireček-line: the approximative border in the antique era between the Latin (north of the line) and the Greek languages

▬ ▬ = the Danubian l i m e s of the Roman empire after 275 AD

········· = present day frontiers

▬ ▬ ▬ = the Carpathian mountains

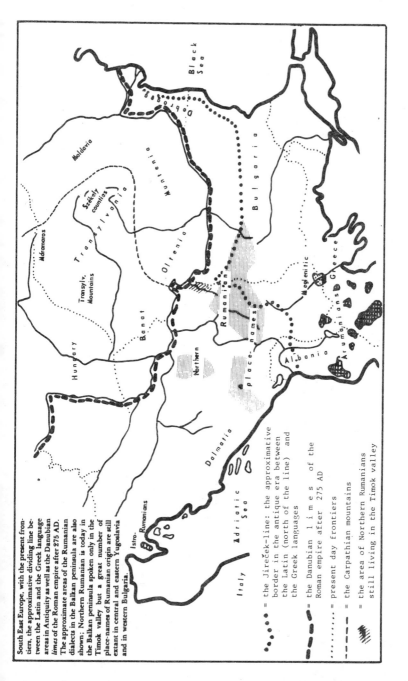 = the area of Northern Rumanians still living in the Timok valley

27

in northern Albania and adjacent areas, the valley of the Black Drin and parts of Old Serbia were the territories of the Albanians during the first centuries AD. E. Cabej, in "Le problème du territoire de la formation de la langue albanaise", Bull, AIESEE, (1972; p. 99), concludes that these territories were the same as present day Albania and, probably for an earlier period of time, also Dardania. *Thus, the ancestors of the Rumanians were living in the mountainous areas of the central parts of the Balkan peninsula, in Old Serbia and adjacent areas.*

6. Summary

Time has come when the theory of continuity, refuted by eminent Rumanian scholars as Ovid Densusianu and having served its original political purpose, should be abandoned and the advent of a new era in Rumanian historical thinking should not be further delayed. The Rumanian people is not served by those who "seek to denature the facts and to deceive themselves" (cf. O. Densusianu, *Histoire de la langue roumaine,* 1901; in the 1975 edition, p. 26; see above, chapter 2) but deserves a balanced, objective and modern description of its troubled past. As regards the legitimate rights of the Rumanians for which so many generations of patriots have fought, these would not be diminished by such a change.

Although not autochthonous in Transylvania, Rumanians have lived at least in some parts of that country for almost 800 years which must be sufficient for that "historical right" which so many historians and politicians tried, wrongly, to derive from a legendary origin from Trajan's soldiers and, the Dacians. This implies the right of living in Transylvania, but *not* the justification of suppressing other nationalities who not only existed earlier in Transylvania but also played a very important role in the development of Rumanian national culture.

There is nothing wrong in emphasizing the positive aspects of the history of one's own nation and to try to bring up the youth in love for their nation and its past. But it is not, as stated by Densusianu, real patriotism to conceal the truth and deceive oneself. The propagation of the theory of continuity conceals many elementary facts and stresses obviously erroneous statements. Meanwhile opposite views, being considered as chauvinistic, are not tolerated. The Rumanians are said to be *the only* people "at home" in South East Europe, all others are called "later colonists", and "strangers". Moreover, Rumanians "never needed anything from strangers and will never need anything from them in the future"? This is a *Herrenvolk*-attitude which denies any other people any place in the land of the Rumanians. How can the *basic human rights* of the other nationalities living in Rumania (about 15% of the total population) be guaranteed in such an atmosphere?

Thus the problem of Roman continuity north of the lower Danube, a question of history and linguistics, is being transformed into an actual conflict not on a juridical but on the cultural and psychological levels. The Rumanians hear and read daily that they belong to a glorious, brave nation which lived and worked and fought in Rumania for several millennia while the members of the national minorities are taught that their ancestors were intruders, accepted by the "Rumanian masses" as colonists and that they, consequently, are not autochthonous in the country, only immigrants, strangers.

And all this is built upon an obsolete, several hundred year old theory which was proven wrong a long time ago.

NOTES

1 Constantinus Porphyrogenitus, 905-959 AD, Byzantine emperor, erudite scholar; cf. *Fontes Historiae Dacoromanae*, II, ed. H. Mihaescu et al., Bucharest, 1970, pp. 656-668.

2 *Istoria României*, ed. C. Daicoviciu, Bucharest, 1960, vol. II, p. 47.

3 Cf., for example, two articles by R. S. Popescu in *Limba română*, Bucharest, XXII, 4, 1973, pp. 309-314 and XXIV, 3, 1975, pp. 263-266; I. Kniezsa, "Kelet-magyarország helynevei" (The place-names in eastern Hungary), in Magyarok és románok, (Hungarians and Rumanians), ed. J. Deér and L. Gáldi, Budapest, 1943, pp. 111-113.

4 *Dicţionar de istorie veche a României*, ed. D. M. Pippidi, Bucharest, 1976, p. 147.

BIBLIOGRAPHY

Alexandru, I. 'Transilvania'. *Tribuna României*; a magazine published by the Association "România", red. P. Chelmez; Bucureşti, VII, No. 127, February 15, 1978, p. 1.

Asztalos, M. (ed.) *A történeti Erdély*. Budapest, 1936 (740 p.).

Barta, G. *Az Erdélyi Fejedelemség születése*; ed. Gondolat, Budapest, 1979 (282 p.).

Çabej, E. *Le problème du territoire de la formation de la langue albanaise*. Bulletin AIESEE, 10, No 2, 1972, pp. 71-99.

Calinescu, G.: *Istoria literaturii române. Compendiu*. Editură pentru literatura, Bucharest, 1968 (429 p.).

Condurachi, E., Daicoviciu, C.: *The Ancient Civilization of Romania*, Barrie and Jenkins, London; Nagel Publishers, Geneva, 1971 (250 p.).

Constantinescu, M. Daicoviciu, C., Pascu, S.: *Istoria României. Compendiu*. Editură didactică si pedagogică, București, 1969 (728 p.).
(Third edition in 1974, ed. S. Pascu. 559 p.)

Curticăpeanu, V.: *Formarea națiunii române si a statului național unitar român*. File de istorie, Editura politică, București, 1974 (92 p.).

Daicoviciu, C.: *Dacica*. Bibliotheca musei Napocensis. Cluj, 1969 (610 p.).

Densusianu, O.: Opere. II: Lingvistica. *Histoire de la langue roumaine*. I. *Les origines*. II. *Le seizieme siècle*. Ed. B. Cazacu, V. Rusu, I. Serb, Editura Minerva, București, 1975, XVIII (1045 p.).

Dimitrescu, Florica (ed.) *Istoria limbii române*; Editură didactică si pedagogică, Bucharest, 1978 (380 p.).

Du Nay, A.: *The Early History of the Rumanian Language*. Edward Sapir Monograph Series in Language, Culture, and Cognition 3. Jupiter Press, Lake Bluff; XI (275 p.), 1977.

Fontes Historiae Dacoromanae, vol. I: ed. V. Iliescu et al; XXIV (791 p.), Edit. Republicii Populare Romîne, București, 1964; vol. II: ed. H. Mihăescu et al., XXII (768 p.), Edit. Republicii Socialiste România, București 1970.

Friedwagner, M.: "Über die Sprache und Heimat der Rumänen in ihrer Frühzeit." *Zeitschrift für romanische Philologie*, Halle, LIV, 1934, pp. 641-715.

Giurescu, C. (ed.): *Istoria României in date*, Editură Enciclopedică Romănă, București, 1971 (525 p.).

Giurescu, C., Giurescu, D.: *Istoria românilor din cele mai vechi timpuri pînă astăzi*, 2nd edition, Editura Albatros, București, 1975 (1038 p.).

Grecu, V.: *Școala Ardeleană și unitatea limbii române literare*. Editura Facla, Timișoara, 1973 (141 p.).

Illyés, E.: *Erdély változása. Mítosz és valóság*. (The Change of Transylvania. Myth and reality.) Aurora, München, 1976, 2nd edition, 426 p. — An English version of this book (National Minorities in Rumania) will appear in 1980.

Iordan, I. (ed.): *Istoria stiințelor in România. Lingvistica*. Editură Academiei Republicii Socialiste România, București, 1975 (175 p.).

Iordan, I.: *Alexandru I. Philippide*. Editură Științifică, București, 1969 (157 p.).

Jancsó, B.: *Erdély története* (The History of Transylvania). Editură Minerva, Cluj-Kolozsvár, 1931 (389 p.).

Kálmán, B.: *The World of Names. A Study in Hungarian Onomatology*; Ed. Akadémiai Kiadó, Budapest, 1978 (199 p.).

Kiss, L.: *Földrajzi nevek etimológiai szótára* (An etymological dictionary of geographical names), Akadémiai Kiadó, Budapest, 1978, pp. 726.

Kniezsa, I.: "Keletmagyarország helynevei", in *Magyarok és románok*, ed. J. Deér and L. Gáldi; Edit. Athenaeum, Budapest, 1943, pp. 111-313.

Maior, P. (ed. F. Fugariu): *Istoria pentru începutul românilor în Dacia*. Vol. I-II. Editura Albatros, București, 1970, vol. I, 279 p., vol. II, 293 p. (A new edition of P. Maior's principal work, published in 1812 in Buda, the Hungarian capital.)

Meier, V.: Ceausescus Freude an den Dakern. Geschichtsthesen und politische Zwecke. *Frankfurter Allgemeine Zeitung*, (West Germany), July 18, 1978.

Pippidi, D. M. (ed.): *Dicționar de istorie veche a României*. Editura Științifică și enciclopedică, București, 1976 (627 p.).

30

Protase, D.: *Problema continuității în Dacia în lumina arheologiei și numismaticii.*
Editură Academiei Republicii Socialiste România, București, 1966, (Biblioteca de arheologie IX), 249 p., (with a summary in French).

Rosetti, Al.: *Istoria limbii române de la origini pînă în secolul al XVII-lea.* Editură pentru literatură, București, 1968 (843 p.).

Rosetti, Al. (ed.): *Istoria limbii române,* vol. I, 1965, Editură Academiei Republicii Populare Române, vol. II, 1969, Editură Academiei Republicii Socialiste România; vol. I, 437 p., vol. II. 464 p.

Russu, I. I.: *Limba traco-dacilor,* (2nd edition), Editură Științifică, București, 1967, 253 p.

Stadtmüller, G. *Forschungen zur albanischen Frühgeschichte.* Albanische Forschungen 2 (2nd edition); Edit. Otto Harrasowitz, Wiesbaden, 1966.

Suciu, C.: *Dicționar istoric al localităților din Transilvania,* vol. I, 1967, 433 p., vol. II, 1968, 447 p.; Editura Academiei Republicii Socialiste România, Bucharest.

Supplex Libellus Valachorum. Translated and commented by K. Köllő; introductory study by I. Pervain and K. Köllő (in Hungarian), Editura Kriterion, București, 1971 (Series Téka), 127 p.

Tamás, L.: *Romains, Romans et Roumains dans l'histoire de Dacie Trajane.* Études sur l'Europe Centre-Orientale I. Budapest, 1936.

THE NATIONALITIES OF DACIA DURING THE ROMAN PERIOD

By

LÁSZLÓ RÉTHY

Published first in the 1886 Annual of the Hungarian Archeological and
Ethnographical Society Budapest

In the first centuries of our era, all the countries surrounding the Mediterranean were subject to the Roman Empire. From Britannia, down the length of the Rhine and Danube to the Black Sea, from the Armenian Highlands to the Tigris and Euphrates, from the Nile to the Atlas Mountains — all were known as "Roman".

With Roman rule, the Latin language extended all over the Empire. The state documents were written in Latin, which also was the language of the army, and in the provinces Celtic, Illyrian, Phrygian, Semitic and Hamitic peoples left inscriptions in the Latin tounge, indicating that for public life the Latin official and literary language held universal sway.

With the expansion of Roman power, the Roman race also spred into the provinces, and from the original Roman parent-tongue new branches evolved: in Iberia the Spanish and Portuguese twin languages, in Gaul Provencal and modern French and in Helvetia Rhaeto-Roman or Romansch.

Many believe that the universal use of Latin brought about the romanisation, i.e. the formation of the new Roman peoples in the conquered barbarian territories, and from this conclude that new Roman peoples sprang up, or could have sprung up in all parts of the Empire, and that the eastern provinces were just as suitable for romanisation as Gaul or Iberia, and if in these territories the romanisation has died out, they attribute this to the barbarian invasions of the fifth century, which swept away the Roman elements, which ranged till Aquincum, Bregetium, Napoca and Potaissa, therefore they believe that the extent of the Roman family of languages is much more restricted today than it was at the time of the Roman Empire. That this belief is erroneous, has not to date been duly emphasised.

Those who are familiar with the Romance languages, and are aware of the relation between them and Latin, will agree with us in that: latinisation and romanisation are two fundamentally different concepts, which should not be confused.

The Latin official language which was spoken and written throughout the provinces was not the language of daily life, and the Romance language did not develop from it, but from the "lingua rustica", the common people's language of Italy. In order for this to have happened, Italian ethnic elements must have settled in the provinces carrying with them their language (lingua rustica) which penetrated the local dialects, thence evolving new languages, new "lingua rustica's".

But the spread of the Italian elements could not keep pace with the rapid expansion of the Empire and only extended to the area surrounding Italy. They spred radially to Hispania, Gaul and to the Alps. The coasts of the Adriatic, to Dalmatia and Albania, everywhere maintaining contact with Italy, which sustained the romanised dialects of these provinces.

Into the further provinces the Italian elements did not penetrate. Thus along the Rhine and the Danube there was no romanisation, neither can we think of it in Pannonia, Dacia, Moesia and further to the east in Asia nor the coast of Africa.

The Egyptian, Celt, Briton, Bregetian, Phoenician or Dolichian who erected altars to his local gods, commemorating his ancestral benefactors, still remained an Egyptian, Celt or Briton who thought in his own language. He was only thinly washed by the official and literary Latin, which never became a factor in his national development.

Those emperors and empresses who originated in Carthage, Syria, Thracia, etc. (Seprimius Severos, Caracalla, Julia Domna, Opelius Macrinus, Antoninus Elagabalus, Philippus Odenathus, Claudius, Aurelianus, Probus, Diocletianus) were latin-speaking Phoenicians, Syrians, Palmyrans, Arabs, or Illyrians but not Romans.

The role of the Latin languages the Roman Empire was exactly the same as the latin of the Middle Ages. In fact it then covered a greater area than in Roman times. The Holy Roman Empire, the English royal court and officials, Swedish, Polish, Czech, Hungarian states and all Christian literature used the Latin language but this did not affect the ethnographical condition of Europe. Latin was the language of the state and the cultured classes, but it was not an ethnographical factor.

During Roman times the imperial boundaries and the extent of the Latin language did not coincide with the full extent of romanisation. Where the legions and fleets stood guard: in long rows on the Rhine and Danube, in the East, in Africa, there were the Roman borders on foreign soil — the Roman eagles represented a boundary of joint institutions and interests, only behind which many nationalities peacefully co-existed. This was an analogous situation to that maintained by the British in Bombay, Calcutta, Hong Kong, Shanghai. Defensive positions.

The last conquest of romanisation was Dacia. This was the furthest removed from Italy of the European colonies. Could the romanisation reach this far? — Bearing in mind the aforegoing discussion, we are forced to conclude in the negative. Let us survey the picture of Roman Dacia.

In A.D. 127 the Emperor Trajan declared war on the Dacian King Decebalus, whose troops had been disturbing the Danubian frontier. Following a war of some year's duration, Dacia became a Roman province.

What people occupied Dacia at this time?

The literary sources name the ruling class Dacians, who were a member of the Thracian-Phrygian family of peoples which lived on the eastern half of the Balkan Peninsula and maintained a connection through Transylvania with the Sarmatians of South Russia and the Jaziges who occupied the area between the Danube and the Theiss. Further members of this family of nations included the Alans of the Trans-Crimea, the Ossetes (Irones) who lived in the Caucasus, the Armenians, Phrygians, Lydians and Bythinians (of Asia Minor). These peoples were all related to the Iranian stock and thus differed from the Illyrians who occupied the Peninsula's Western half prior to the Iranian Thracian-Dacian-Scythian group, in the era of the aryan influx. They also differed in language from this latter group. [1]

At the time of Trajan the Thracian-Dacian-Scythian National group was in a process of dissolution. The Slavs had broken their barriers. In South Russia the Slavs had reached the Black Sea, other groups had reached Transylvania, even as far as Orsova on the Danube. This can be deduced from Transylvania's Roman period topography. The river names "Czerna" "Berzovia" could only have come from the Slav: the one means "black" and the other, "swift", in all Slavic dialects.

The Dacian element was strongest on the Rumanian Plains, and this is borne out by the numerous place names terminating in — "Dava", found there during the Roman period.

It seems certain that by the time of Trajan's conquest, a numerically strong Slavic population lived in Dacia, and was supplanting the indigenous Dacians.

By his conquests Trajan extended the frontiers of the Empire to the Carpathian Mountains. A "vallum" was erected on the Russian Plains between the river Pruth and the sea, later being extended from the Pruth to the Dniester.

Numerous colonies were founded in the new province, mostly superseding older local settlements. However, some were established in previously unsettled areas, mining districts.[2]

The colonies in Transylvania comprised: Napoca (Kolozsvár), Pataissa (Torda), Sarmizegethusa (Vásárhely), Apulum (Gyulafehérvár), Alburnus Major (Abrudbánya, Verespatak), Ampelum (Zalatna) Salinea, Brucla (Marosújvár, Nagyenyed), Porolissum (Mojgrad), Largiana (Zutor), Resculum (Sebesváralja), Optatiana (Magyargorbó), Cedoniae (Szeben).

In the Danube Valley: Ad Mediam (Mehadia), Tsierna (Orsova), Berzovia.

The pattern of Roman life in Dacia resembled that in other parts of the Empire. A cultured, civilized way of life; cities of stone, amphitheatres, baths, aquaducts and temples.

The population however was not of Italian origin to the slightest degree.

For Italians, Dacia was a distant land with an unpleasant climate. Also, by this period Italy was an exhausted land that had no surplus population.

From literary and palaeographic sources it is known that the Roman population of Dacia comprised peoples from all over the Empire, although mainly from Asia Minor, and if Italian elements were present, they were only a very insignificant minority.

According to Eutropius (VIII. 3) "Traianus victa Dacia ex toto orbe romano infinitas eo copias hominum transtulerat ad agros et colendas."[3]

What Eutropius states in general, is confirmed in detail by inscriptions. From these we know that the Roman colonists of Dacia were mainly of Semitic origin, i.e. Syrians, Palmyrans, Bythinians, Commageneites and Galatians. There also were Celts, Greeks and, as miners Pyrusteans from South-Dalmatia.

This multi-lingual population was scattered over the Dacian and Slavic area. Most of them understood Latin or Greek, but at home they spoke the language of their respective country of origin, and lived according to their native civilization.

Let us analyse the ethnographic situation of these colonists in the light of the inscription-derived information.

The provincial capital, Ulpia Traiana Sarmizegethusa exhibits various national groups: one part of the population probably was of native Dacian (Slavic?) origin. One inscription mentions a Dacian name (C.I.L. 1385), "Bovipal" which seems to belong to the Scythian and Jazig languages which had names ending in "pala" or "pal". A native origin seems indicated also by the religious monuments: "I.O.M. Terrae Daciae, Dii Deae Daciarum, Genus Daciarum" (C.I.L. 1351, 1063, 993).[4]

Greeks also lived in Sarmizegethusa, as attested by a Latin-Greek inscription (C.I.L. 1422). Also indicating Greek colonists is a mithras altar dedicated by one Anicetus (C.I.L. 1436) and the temple to Aesculapius and Hygiea (C.I.L. 1417) a).

However, most of the population of Sarmizegethusa was of Syrian origin, as evidenced by the numerous Mithras monuments, and other at Várhely is inscribed the name "MALAGBEL", a god of Syrian-Phoenician derivation.

Another monument, in the museum at Deva lists a number of Semita gods, "MALAGBEL", "BEBELLAHAMON", "BENEFAL and MANAVAT".

To the north of the capital lays the colony of Germisara

(Algyógy). This also was occupied by people from Asia Minor, but Galatians, not Semites. This is proven by the presence of a "Collegium Galatarum".

Near Germisara was Apulum (Gyulafehérvár). The name is analogous to Apulia, but it was not settled by Apulians. The population comprised Greeks, Palmyrans, Syrians, Paphlagonians, Celts, people from the Alps and from Emesa in Syria.

An inscription (C.I.L. 1108) mentions the sun god of the Palmyrans, Hierobolus by name. The cult of the Emesians is commemorated by a number of monuments (C.I.L. 1030-1138), and the Paphlagonians with their god Abonutichos by two inscriptions (C.I.L. 1021, 1022).

In the district of Apulum, where today lie Alvincz, Marosnémeti, Déva and Nagyenyed, the ethnographic picture is very varied.

In Alvincz are traces of Greeks (Ephemeridis 412) and at Marosnémeti and Déva, Syrians who sacrificed to Jupiter Heliopolitanus (C.I.L. 1353-54) between Nagyenyed and Gyulafehérvár another Syrian nation the Delicheians left a monument of their god Jupiter Dolicheius (Ephemeridis 400). They are also mentioned on an inscription found at Maros Portus (Ephem. 401).

Past Apulum in the mountains, the mining towns of Ampelum, Saliane and Alburnus Major were the more important settlements where Pyrustan and Dalmatian miners operated the salt and gold mines. (C.I.L. III. Tabulae Ceratae and inscription 1323.) Besides them, the mining towns were occupied by Greeks, Dolicheans, Commageneites (both Semitic people) and Bythinians (C.I.L. 1301, 1324). An inscription mentions two priests of the Dolicheans and Commageneites, Addebar, Semei and Oceanus Socratis.

Thus it can be seen that the heart of Dacia was occupied by a very diverse population. To the north the situation was similar.

In Potaissa (Torda) we again find Greeks, Syrians and Palmyrans. An inscription mentions the goddess Isis Myrionyma who was worshipped by the Greeks, whilst the Syrians raised an altar to the God Aziz the companion of the sun-god, who was a figure of the cult of Emesa in Syria (C.I.L. 875, 1138). Here in Potaissa was also found a monument to the Numerus Palmyrenorum, an army unit of Syrian origin, thus containing numerous Syrian personal names. (Torma, revidirte und neue Inschriften zu C.I.L. III. Wien 1881 4. p.)

Equally, or more mixed was the population of Napoca (Kolozsvár), the capital of Northen Dacia. The inhabitants included Galatians from Tavia (C.I.L. 860), Dolicheans (Ephemerides 373), Carians (C.I.L. 859), and other Asiatics. A name-list of the latter is extant (C.I.L. 870). In 235 they had a collegium, headed by a "Spirarcha".

The stele called "NOMINA ASIANORUM" (Zoilianus scripsit) includes typical non-Roman names such as Tattario, Dizo, Hyius, Zoilus Zoilianus, Eptala, Suri, Tzinto, Greca, Ermes, Asclepiodate, etc.

Towards the Carpathians the settlements thin out but in the vicinity of Marosvásárhely, between Mikháza and Deményháza, there was found an inscription concerning a ship-hiring Collegium, the business of which extended all over Dacia. This Collegium was not Italian either, the cult of Adrastea named in the inscription (C.I.L. 944) indicates Asians from Mysia and Phrygia.

Towards the lower Danube the "Colonia Zernensium" and "Berzovia" take their names from Slavic inhabitants. The cult of Jupiter Cerneunus indicates an unbroken occupation by the native inhabitants.

Near Karánsebes we again find Dolicheans and Palmyrans. One inscription is dedicated to Jupiter Dolicheus (Ephem. 443), and another commemorates in Latin and Palmyrene language, an optio names Flavius Guras. This was offered by Aelius Habibis, the priest of the local Palmyrans. This monument highlights the close contact between the Asiatics in Dacia and how much, in spite of romanization they remained Asians at heart. The stone is inscribed in Latin, but underneath it lists the donors rank and name (Guru Ben Jaddai optio) in Palmyran characters.

The army's composition was as heterogeneous as the colonies. The legions in Trajan's time and even more so later, were made up from the most diverse peoples from all over the known world. The Dacian Garrison was also like this: the soldiers included Illyrians, Pannonians, Spaniards, Britons, Numidians, Egyptians and men from the Alps.

Upon such an ethnographic basis, a new Roman nation,

such as in Gaul or Spain, could not form in Dacia. If a new language had evolved, it would more likely have been Semitic than Roman. But whatever language would have formed in Dacia this should have left a trace in today's language, because languages retain, in fossilised form, an indication of what various tounges they had evolved from.

The theory that a new people and language had evolved in Dacia has to be abandoned. Ethnologically it is an invalid assumption because Roman life in Dacia was very shortlived and its people later dispersed in the other Balkan provinces or returned to Asia.

In the 3rd century Dacia was threatened by the Goths. These people had come from the Baltic, and traversing Lithuania and Poland, eventually arrived in the Crimea, surrounding Dacia in the process. The Huns followed the Goths preceded by displaced German elements who thus were forced to invade Dacia.

The situation in Dacia soon became untenable. Aurelian withdrew the settlers and garrison, resettling them in Moesia which henceforth was renamed Dacia Aureliana.

According to Flavius Vopiscus, Sextus, Rufus and Eutropius, the entire Roman population was evacuated. Eutropius states (IX. 15): "Provinciam Daciam intermisit vastato omni Illyrico et Moesia desperans eam posse retineri abductosque Romanos ex urbibus et agris Daciae in media Moesiae collocavit appellavitque eam Daciam, quae nunc in duas Moesias dividit et est in dextera Danubio in mare fluenti, cum antea fuerit in laeva."[5]

With the age of Aurelian the one and a half century (107-260) story of Roman Dacia comes to an end. Minting ceased in 257.

The last Latin inscriptions date from 257-260, and even numismatic remains do not go beyond Aurelian.

The Roman civilization was destroyed. The very names of cities were lost, as there was no one living in Dacia to remember. The mines were abandoned by the Pyrusteans. It was only in the 18th cent. that the "tabula ceratas" hidden by the Greek and Dalmatian miners at Alburnus Major against a better time, were discovered. The better times never came.

According to the literary and archeological sources, to the best of knowledge Dacia completely ceased to be Roman. The Danube again became the frontier of the Empire. Viminatium (Kosztolacz), Egeta (Palanka), Bononia (Viddin), Ratiaria (Arcar), Durostorum (Silistria), became the stations of the legions guarding the border.

That any Romans remained in Dacia after the time of Aurelian is an impossibility. The peasantry of the Roman period continued to inhabit the land, as they did during the German period. This population, however was Slavic. This can be seen from the fact that the names of Dacian towns completely disappeared but the names of Rivers of Slavic origin continued, and flourished down to modern times.

The Rumanian nationalistic studies to establish the origin of the Rumanian language in Dacia can thus be seen to be based on erroneous assumptions. No Rumanian language was born in Dacia; it could only have originated in an area of romanisation, and in this area this only happened in Dalmatia. Thus the birth-place of the Rumanian language is Dalmatia. The whole character of the language points at an Illyrian origin and it indicates the Roman history of Dalmatia.

(Translated by GEORGE VASS)

NOTES

1 The Illyrians are the first wave of Aryans in Europe. Italy's pre-Latin and Greece's pre-Hellene population belonged to this race.

2 The colonization of Dacia was on restricted lines, occupying mainly the area extending from the Marosh Valley to the Hátszeg district and north to Kolozsvár. The Rumanian plain was only sparsely colonised.

3 Translation. "Trajan, after he was victorious in Dacia, transferred a great number of people from the whole Roman Empire to work on the fields of Dacia."

4 Translation. "Territory of Dacia. The Gods and Godesses and people of Dacia. The people of the Dacians."

5 Translation. "He (Aurelian) left Dacia. After the devastation of the whole Illyria and Moesia he tried at least to retain Moesia. Thus he relocated the Romans taken out from the cities and countryside of Dacia in Moesia. He renamed Moesia: Dacia, which from now on was divided in two parts: one of them was on the right side of the Danube approaching the sea, the other, the older one being on the left side of the river."

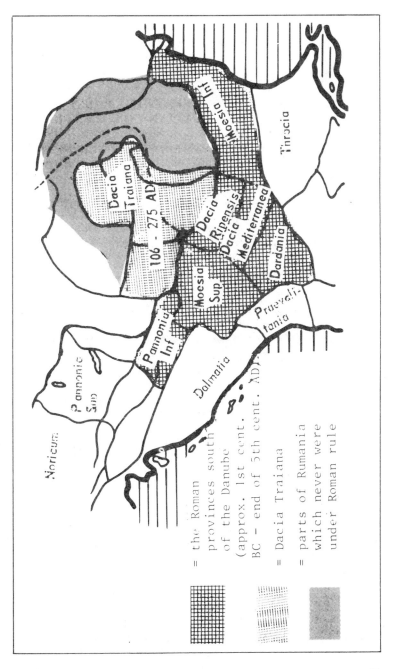

= the Roman provinces south of the Danube (approx. 1st cent. BC – end of 5th cent. AD).

= Dacia Traiana

= parts of Rumania which never were under Roman rule

WHO WERE THE PEOPLE
LIVING IN THE CARPATHIAN BASIN
BEFORE THE HUNGARIAN CONQUEST?

Interest in early history of the Hungarians and of the peoples of the Danube region in general – has greatly increased in Hungary recently. Unlike in Rumania, however, historical curiosity in Hungary has distinguished itself by a realistic reappraisal of the past. Myths are being discarded and reality is being discovered by the newest means of modern scholarship. An example of this trend is the round-table discussion on the peoples of the Carpathian Basin before the Hungarian conquest in the 9th century. It was originally broadcast by the Hungarian Radio. In 1979, it was published in the first issue of a new magazine, *Historia*, serving the general public. The participants of this discussion are all prominent scholars and professors, leading authorities in their fields: György Györffy, Péter Hanák, László Makkai, and András Mócsy.

Péter Hanák:

A century ago, or even fifty years ago, records of the era of Hungarian conquest in the consciousness of Hungarians were tied to Etelköz, Verecke, and Pusztaszer. Today these names are gradually receding into the realm of literature, while in Hungarian historical consciousness their place is being taken by Vértesszöllős, Fenékpuszta, and Szabolcs. Historical knowledge and interest has changed fundamentally in recent decades. Myth has been replaced by excavation. Public law, which virtually dominated political historiography, has been replaced by new approaches of social and cultural history. Interest has shifted away from the heroic deeds of the chieftains and turned toward the culture-building activity of the peoples of the Danubian Basin. This change is also characterized by greater emphasis upon exact demonstration and respect for facts. The attempt to obtain meaning from stones, bones, and tools, has become paramount.

András Mócsy:

The discoveries of archeologists have undoubtedly provided historians with information which, when compared with the sporadic and metastatic written and linguistic traditions, can be considered objective. Materials which are discovered by archeology, quite obviously, were not left intentionally for posterity. Those who left these materials behind did not wish to make a statement about themselves. These "remnants," whether in form of graves, or signs of someone having lived there, simply remained because they existed.

Hanák:

What does the archeological knowledge of this era tell us about the centuries before the Hungarian conquest, about the Hungarians of the era of conquest, and generally about the people who lived in our homeland at that time?

Mócsy:

We have information about cultures and peoples of the Roman era and the early Middle Ages. There are cultures we can associate with people, and we know which people; however, we also have knowledge of cultures which we cannot as yet associate with a specific group of people. In general, cultures can be best characterized by ages rather than by peoples. The question of relationship between culture and ethnicity brings about intense debates. However, archeology possesses another secure anchor and that is settlement. In that connection one might make reference to Fenékpuszta or to Tác, one of the most significant Trans-Danubian archeological sites, also mention might be made of my most recent dig at Tokod. In each case the continuity of settlement existed in the midst of two contemporaneous but distinct cultures, between which there were no signs of continuity. There were settlements which remained even after the demise of a great historical epoch, such as the Roman area settlement of Fenékpuszta which significantly outlived that age. However, there occured a sharp break in the fifth century. During the most recent excavations, a mass grave was discovered which contained the remains of a number of individuals who had been left unburied for at least a half year, if no longer, after their death; this points to an obvious and sharp break with continuity. Another and different example of continuity was the Tokod fortress, where a small and, in terms of their patterns of life, well-defined, Romanized people lived in a Roman era settlement, undisturbed until the end of the fifth century.

However, what we can responsibly state today is that in the eight and ninth centuries we know of no archeologically definable culture or settlement in the Carpathian Basin which can be traced back to Roman times. Conversely, we know of no settlement which existed in such a manner in the eighth and ninth centuries that it could trace back its existence continuously to the earlier centuries, specifically the Roman era. What peoples lived here in the eighth and ninth centuries? We must first think of the Avars, specifically in relation to that culture which the archeologists, perhaps with excessive circumspection, define as Avar-era rather than Avar. We can also think of the Slavs; however, with them it is especially interesting that in the eighth and ninth centuries we cannot speak of a single Slavic culture; instead mention can be made of numerous such archeologically definable cultures, among which one ot the other, with greater or lesser certainty, can be attributed to the Slavs or also to the Slavs.

György Győrffy:

A seventh century Byzantine source permits us a glance at the ethnic affiliation of the peoples who lived here. As a consequence of the war between Byzantium and the Avars, the Byzantines captured 8800 warriors, among them 3000 Avars, 3000 Gepids, 800 Slavs, and 2000 barbarians, in all likelihood Bulgarians. This mirrors the ethnic character of the Carpathian Basin in the seventh century. During the era of migration, the Gepids occupied the eastern half of the Carpathian Basin and Transylvania; they never left that area and yet disappeared by the ninth century just as the Avars did. There is an old Russian proverb about this: "They disappeared just as the Avars did."

Mócsy:

Yes, one could cite other examples of such disappearances. For example, the Sarmatians occupied for nearly four centuries practically the entire Hungarian lowlands (the Alföld); although two of their leaders are mentioned in the sources even after the destruction of the empire of the Huns in the fifth century, after that one can find no further mention of them in the sources. In such cases one is not speaking about a catastrophic destruction of peoples, but rather that the social life of a group of people has been so disarranged that it cannot maintain it even on the primitive tribal level and thus it can be more easily assimilated, perhaps even by a change of language.

Hanák:

There has been no mention thus far of a people which played an important role during the Roman era, namely the Dacians. It is true that our knowledge concerning them relates to their existence in the first century B.C. and first to third centuries A.D. The Dacian state, which spread throughout Transylvania and the lower Danube region, was conquered by Trajan at the beginning of the second century and was under Roman rule for altogether 170 years. (This was a substantially shorter period than the 400 years of Roman rule over Pannonia.) The question, therefore, is as follows: Were the Dacians destroyed during this 170 years or did they maintain themselves as a Romanized people until the third century, when the Romans moved out of the eastern provinces as a consequence of the numerous Gothic incursions.

Mócsy:

The situation with the Dacians is the same as with the other indigenous population of the Roman era. It is a matter of common knowledge that the Romans nowhere brought into being a "tabula rasa" and certainly did not engage in the destruction of native populations. Nonetheless, the indigenous populations of the Roman provinces disappeared together with the end of Roman rule. The Illyrian and the Celtic natives were assimilated in the same manner as the Sarmatians and obviously the Dacians shared this fate; they did not outlive the era of Roman rule. As a people and as an ethnic group they disappeared.

László Makkai:

Permit me to cite a recently deceased outstanding Rumanian historian and archeologist, Constantin Daicoviciu. In one of his works published shorthly before his death — fundamentally in agreement with the observations of András Mócsy — he stated the following: "The second half of the fifth century witnessed the beginning of deep troubles (in the territory of Transylvania also—my observation) and every settlement large or small known to be Daco-Roman, seemed to be empty. (I must myself add that this was the case from an archeological point of view.) The autochtonous Daco-Roman peoples did not demonstrate their presence in the archeological remains and thus one is really faced with the temporary absence of these peoples from their settlements; they moved back into the mountains. Only after the passage of a certain time, which could not have been very long, did the original inhabitants return to those settlements which had, in the meanwhile, been conquered by the Slavs beginning in the eighth century." Thus Daicoviciu, the outstanding Rumanian archeologist, also states that on the entire territory of historic Hungary, including Transylvania, the continuity of peoples had been broken.

Hanák:

I cannot keep silent a seemingly serious methodological observation. To what extent may one identify archeological evidence with an ethnic group? In his introductory observations András Mócsy spoke rather about cultures and settlements which were not always identifiable with ethnic groups. Well, can we tie it to a specific ethnic group in this instance?

Mócsy:

We must know from written historical sources in what territory a people lived at a specific time. If the concrete archeological culture extends to the same territory at the same time, then the identification is permitted. One of the difficulties facing the researcher is that the archeologically specified cultures are either smaller or larger than one or another ethnic unit. The other difficulty is that an archeologically defined culture or object does not speak. Therefore the determination, let us say, what language was spoken by the user of an object is the responsibility of linguistic history.

Győrffy:

Certainly an archeologist cannot make a skeleton speak, just as it is impossible to determine what language a dead person laid out in contemporary European dress spoke or to which ethnic group he belonged without some telltale sign. However, this is precisely what most interests the scholar. This question cannot be answered by archeology, but only by historical sources; this must be emphasized in any decision concerning the history of the movement of peoples, because contemporary man has a tendency to view the ethnic groupings of the Middle Ages through the same glasses with which he views peoples and nations today. He does this in spite of the fact that the consciousness of peoples in the Middle Ages was manifested in different ways. Europe at the time of the migration of peoples was a great ethnic melting pot in which the different tribes had not as yet solidified definitively into peoples; a war inevitably brought entirely new groupings, often with different names, into being. This is why it is, especially in the case of Eastern Europe — and most evidently in the Byzantine sources — that constantly changing ethnic designations appear and we cannot decide which peoples were later referred to by such ethnic designations. If we examine which peoples have had a role in the territory known as East Central Europe since the first millenium (such as Poles, Hungarians, Croatians) and then search for these peoples on an ethnic map reflecting an earlier period, we will be shocked to learn that these peoples either did not exist or were located elsewhere and lived under different circumstances.

Hanák:

What György Györffy has said about the ethnic relations of the migrations of the fifth through tenth centuries and the ethno-geneticism of the early Middle Ages, only strengthens the methodological concern expressed earlier. Is the theory of the double conquest, which has elicited so much controversy among historians and archeologists the past few years, acceptable on the basis of this argument? Is it possible to substantiate the theory that the late Avar archeological findings actually masked the participants to an earlier "first" conquest of Hungary, given the uncertainties of the ethnic explanation of such findings.

Györffy:

From the aforesaid it follows that the substantiation of this is very difficult, indeed almost impossible. The archeologists uncovered large graveyards which contained large numbers of artifacts characterized by griffin and tendril ornamentation; from the findings it is possible to ascertain that we are faced with the remnants of a people comprised mainly of mounted horsemen, although they were also acquainted with the rudiments of agriculture. From the layers it is generally possible to determine the era to which the culture belonged, in which century it appeared, and how long it lasted, but it is simply not possible to make archeological findings speak; nor do these findings reveal what language these peoples spoke nor to what ethnic group they belonged.

Makkai:

There is a Byzantine source from app. 670 according to which the Bulgarian tribal confederation living on the steppe lands along the Black Sea disintegrated and one part migrated to the Carpathian basin. Might there have been Hungarians among these people?

Győrffy:

It has long been known that among the subjects of the Avar empire were various Ogur-Turkish and Bulgarian tribes. The Danube Bulgarians were also Ogur Turks, who were also known as Onogurs or Onogundur Bulgarians. This Onogur designation was nothing more than the name used by foreigners to designate the Magyars. (It was used in different versions such as ongr, ungr, hungarus, ungar.) Thus, our ethnic name can be traced back to the Bulgarian-Turkish Onogur designation. This, however, does not mean that every Onogur people spoke the Finno-Ugrian language, since we know specifically that the Danubian Onogur-Bulgarians spoke a distinct Bulgarian-Turkish dialect; numerous texts of their language have survived. We can consider it to be a proven fact that during the Avar era such a Bulgarian-Turkish people moved into the Carpathian basin; they had a role in the development of the Hungarians, but we cannot state that the Bulgarian-Turkish element which came spoke a Finno-Ugrian language; furthermore, we cannot state that they determined the ethnic-linguistic structure of the Carpathian basin.

Hanák:

László Makkai made reference to a written record. Until now we have rather gathered together the archeological material supportive of these positions. However, we must associate and confront these findings with the lessons derived from these Byzantine, Arab, and German sources which have been known for at least a century and subjected to critical scrunity in the past.

Mócsy:

In connection with the Byzantine sources I wish to mention three examples, which will also illuminate the three methods of source criticism. One of these is the account of Priskos, an important source for the history of the Huns. He wrote very graphically about the court of Attila. The reason the work is very significant and a very dependable source is because Priskos reported as an eye-witness; he had undertaken an official trip to the Carpathian basin. (He visited here as a political envoy in the mid-fifth century.) He wrote that the people living north of the Danube spoke the language of the Huns and the Goths and that only those knew Latin who engaged in the Balkan trade with the Romans.

The author of the other Byzantine source was Prokopios, the last great figure of Greek historical writing in the sixth century. However, what Prokopios wrote about the Carpathian basin was pure speculation, written mostly at his desk without the benefit of first-hand observation. For example, he wrote that the territory north of the Danube was completely unpopulated; however, we know from other sources exactly which peoples lived there.

Finally, mention should be made of the third category of sources. Numerous chronologies provide information about the history of the Avar-Byzantine wars; these are mostly quite sketchy and provide only brief statements about some of the events.

Győrffy:

The other collections of sources only give one or two brief references about the peoples who lived there, most often in connection with some military conflict or political event.

Numerous contemporary sources took note of the Hungarian conquest and mention was made of those peoples who fought alongside the Hungarians; the Fulda Chronicles, for example, mentioned the Bulgarians, Moravians, and Franks. I wish to call special attention to the Mohammedan sources, most written in Arabic and a small number in Persian. These provided a trade-inspired geography for the territories frequented by merchants, including also information about the peoples living in the area of the Black Sea, the boundaries of the Magyar-populated Etelköz region, and the boundaries and neighboring peoples generally. They state that at the Danube the Bulgarians (also known as Nándorok) were the neighbors of the Magyars; furthermore, these sources also reveal that between the Bulgarians—whose rule extended to the southern half of the great Hungarian Plain (Alföld)—and the Moravians there was unsettled land so wide that it took a ten days' journey to cross it. After this, these sources turned their attention to the Slavs in such a way that on the basis of these descriptions we obtain also information about the large numbers of Cinikumans in the Danube valley.

If we compare the Arab sources with some similar Western European geographical accounts, the picture becomes even clearer. During the 830's a Bavarian geographer reported on the peoples living north of the Danube; he identified them not only by tribe, but also stated how many *civitas* were included in their territory; (a *civitas* was a region around a fortress; one *civitas* was equivalent to one clan). We are informed that the Bulgarians possessed five *civitas* north of the Danube. He mentioned the Magyars of Etelköz; however, no mention was made of those peoples who arrived in this region only later, such as the Petschenegs, Cumans, and Vlachs.

Hanák:

We have reviewed the significant and most accepted sources, namely the Byzantine, Arab, and German ones. There are, however, some Magyar sources, which have as their major theme the conquest era and the situation of that time. This major source is Anonymus. He influenced not only the Hungarian historical consciousness, but also Hungarian historiography. His influence can be gauged on the basis of these two examples. The 1975 Hungarian language facsimile edition of Anonymus, published in 12,000 copies, was completely sold out in four weeks. (Since then a new edition has also been sold out.) The other fact is that not only in our scholarly tradition, but also in the historical scholarship of our neighbors—in Slovakia and Rumania—it is a fundamental source, indeed even a bible for this purpose. Hence, where do we stand regarding the critical value of Anonymus?

Győrffy:

We must not forget that the writer Magister P., known as Anonymus, lived 300 years after the era of the Hungarian conquest; he had no written sources about the event as the modern historian does. If he consulted older materials, he turned first to the Bible or some ancient writer (such as the account of the Scythians by Justinian), but he possessed only very few and scant sources about the conquest era itself. This being granted, he wished to present an interesting account of the conquest based upon a literary form widespread in twelfth century France. This literary form grew out of the culture of chivalry and through it they wished to revive in an enthralling manner those histories which were read at court and reaped a great success there. This literary form was the romantic gesta. As the "romantic" appelation indicates, its author did not strive to engage in critical historical scholarship, but rather wished to entertain. However, there was in Anonymus a significant social message for his age. He presented numerous Hungarian heroes in his pages and in many cases mentioned that the descendants of these heroes were still living and working on that land their ancestors had conquered. Anonymus recounted these episodes of the conquest in a very interesting and colorful manner. He also presented these episodes throughout his work, pointing out how a certain leader conquered that land which his descendants now owned. It was in this that his work spoke meaningfully to his contemporaries. We must somehow imagine that Anonymus, as Béla III's notary, was well acquainted with the aristocratic circles and thus was in a position to listen to the stories recounted by the aristocrats about their ancestors; from these he attempted to put together some kind of romantic gesta. Since these ever-changing oral family traditions (over a 300 year period) have no significant historical source value, Anonymus has no authentic source value.

Hanák:

This conclusion can be found in the introduction to the new edition of Anonymus, also written by György Győrffy. Thus, Anonymus flashed back the family, gentilitial, and property relations of his own age to the era of conquest. This is demonstrated by the fact that he presented such peoples in his work who were either not there at the time of the conquest or can no longer be found in the Carpathian basin. On the one hand, he spoke of the fact that after the death of Attila the Romans conquered this territory and the Hungarians supposedly battled with the Romans at Veszprém. On the other hand, he placed the Cumans into Hungary in the ninth century, even though they only arrived there in the eleventh century. The confounding of facts and the confusion of chronology characterizes the Gesta of Anonymus in much the same manner as the ahistorical and retrospective presentations of other chroniclers.

Makkai:

There is, however, an interesting feature about Anonymus we have not mentioned as yet; he enjoyed engaging in linguistics. He connected a whole series of personal names with placenames, even if he did so only by employing his imagination. The recently deceased outstanding personality of Hungarian linguistic scholarship, István Kniezsa, established a theoretically useful and methodologically outstanding system for research into placenames. This system extended to placenames and river names. On the basis of this modern linguistic scholarship, what was the appearance of the Carpathian basin around 1000 A.D.? The researches indicate that there were three categories of river names. One of these categories comprised the following: Szamos, Maros, Kőrös, Tisza, Dráva, Száva, Temes, Duna, and Rába; without exception these date back to Roman times or to even earlier eras, but there is one problem. These are all designations about which nothing else can be proven except that these terms entered both the Hungarian and Rumanian languages through Slavic mediation. Thus these river designations did not come directly from Roman, and even less from Pannonian, Illyrian, or other peoples, into the language of the Hungarians, Rumanians, or Germans living here, but were taken over from the Slavs. The mid-sized and smaller river designations originated only from those people about whom we have information from the beginning of the ninth century; concretely these would be the Hungarians and the Slavs. First a series of Slavic examples: Beszterce, Zsitva, Rábca . . . and the list could be continued. There is an interesting, peculiar, and specific type among them, such as the Küküllő-Ternava designation; thus we have a dual designation. The Küküllő means "Kökényes" and the Slav word Ternava means the same thing. In an interesting manner, the Rumanians took over the Ternava designation from the Slavs living there, while the Hungarians took over the word of Turkic origin, namely Küküllő, but used another word with the same meaning to make the designation. In addition to these Slavic placenames, the entire Carpathian basin was characterized by a preponderance of Hungarian place designations, such as Ér, Berrettyo, Aranka, but let us also mention some typical ones such as Nyárád, Lápos, Aranyos — in Transylvania; in Rumanian, for example, the terms Nyárád and Nyirázs are borrowings from the older form of the Hungarian Nyárágy; Lápos became Lopus, also a borrowing from Hunharian, and Aranyos became Arics, another borrowing from Hungarian. Therefore, the mid-sized and smaller rivers were already named by those peoples who still live there now.

Győrffy:

Yes, that is the case with river designations, but the situation is different with another category of placenames, namely the designations of villages, cities, and fortresses. Those who research the origin of the names of settlements often consider the current designations as the legacy of some long lost people. On the basis of the most resent research, the settlement designations of historic Hungary can generally not be traced back to the era before the conquest. We can prove this by pointing out that the conquering Hungarians captured the territories east and north of the Danube in fierce battles from the Bulgarians and Moravians, while Pannonia fell to them virtually without struggle. We should expect, therefore, that the settlement designations of Pannonia would have remained and lived on in Hungarian placenames. This, however, did not occur; every settlement designation dates back only to the post-conquest era. This seems to indicate that settlement designations are not suitable for demonstrating any kind of continuity.

Hanák:

During the course of a lengthy discussion, we have spoken of the new results of archeology, historical source criticism, and linguistic scholarship and have substantially come to the conclusion that no continuity can be demonstrated between the populations of the former provinces of the Roman Empire and the peoples who lived there in the ninth century, 500 years later. The continuity — whether it involved a relationship with the Huns, the idea of the "Great Moravian Empire", or descent from the Dacians — was invented by chroniclers and historians; it was they who provided a historical coloring for the ancient legends and myths.

These myths were raised to a level of scholarly respectability only by the romantic historiography of the early nineteenth century, in order to awaken the nation, foster an interest in the heroic past, and engage in the romantic idealization of this past. In this capacity they undoubtedly achieved something positive of a propagandistic nature 150-200 years ago during the era of national awakening. Scholarship, however, has advanced beyond myth; indeed, a true self-awareness — one might even say a Danube-region self-awareness — directly demands a historical critique of such myths. We will be able to resonstruct the era of the movement of peoples in our common historical region, namely the Danube basin, in terms of the ethnic and cultural relations, with scholarly objectivity and a sense of realism only if we free scholarship from the intent of providing a legally conditioned historical defense of the current political condition. The international and regional political relations of this region will, in any case, not be decided on the basis of indigeneity or historical priorities.

(Translated by THOMAS SZENDREY)

LA VERSION LA PLUS RECENTE
DE LA THEORIE DE LA CONTINUITE
DACO-ROUMAINE (1 re partie)

Par

JEAN CSONKA

Sous les auspices de l'Académie des Sciences Sociales et Politiques et de l'Académie de la République Socialiste de Roumanie, Miron Constantinescu et Stefan Pascu, membres de l'Académie, et le Dr. Petre Diaconu ont publié un volume en anglais, concernant le problème de la continuité daco-roumaine. Le livre: *Relations Between the Autochthonous Population and the Migratory Populations on the Territory of Rumania* (Bucarest, 1975, 323 pages) présente 21 études écrites par des spécialistes roumains(*).

1. Dans l'introduction du livre, S. Pascu déclare: "La formation du peuple roumain était déjà achevée, sa langue latine formée en tant que vocabulaire et structure grammaticale, et son organisation politique assez avancée ('pretty advanced') lorsque, apres s'être fixée sur la plaine de la-Pannonie en 896, une partie de la population hongroise commence à pénétrer en Transylvanie dans la première moitié du Xe siècle, pour y rencontrer la ferme résistance des armées mises sur pied par des voïévodes roumains ou roumano-slaves ('Slavic') dans la région des rivières Körös, dans le Banat et le plateau Transylvain;

(*) La théorie de la continuité daco-roumaine a produit une littérature abondante. Il n'entre pas dans l'intention de la présente étude d'étaler tous les aspects du problème et toutes les opinions. "The studies contained in the present volume are intended to clarify some intricate and complex issues long debated by scholars", dit S. Pascu, co-éditeur du livre ("Relations . . .", p. 11). Apparemment, le but du livre est de présenter au monde les résultats des recherches intenses entreprises après la Deuxième Guerre Mondiale, pendant un quart de siècle, de 1950 à 1975 environ. Il s'agit avant tout des recherches archéologiques et de leur interprétation.
La place disponible réduite d'un périodique a rendu inévitable que les parties relevantes du livre soient seulement données en traduction française — sans donner le texte original en anglais — mais aussi fidèlement que possible, d'où parfois un texte français déficient.

lorsque vers la fin du Xe siècle l'Empire Byzantin étend son hégémonie sur le cours inférieur du Danube face à l'opposition des 'puissants' de ces régions''.

"Pendant le 2e millénaire av. J.-C., une série de mutations ethniques ont eu lieu en Asie et en Europe — dit Vladimir Iliescu dans la première étude, p. 13. Un des groupes les plus grands et les plus nombreux, à côté des Celtes, Iraniens et Indiens, étaient les Thraces qui se fixèrent au nord de la Mer Noire, sur le territoire de la Roumanie et sur une grande partie des Balkans. Dans une note il cite Hérodote: "Le peuple thrace est le plus nombreux au monde après les Indiens".

2. C'est Hadrian Daicoviciu qui décrit dans son étude: "*Daces et Romains dans la province de Trajan*" (pages 35-53) comment les Daces de la colonie romaine de Dacie sont devenus "Roumains" de nos jours. Le lecteur est prié de bien vouloir distinguer entre Romain de Rome et de l'Empire Romain, d'un côté, et Roumain (Romeni, Rumeni, Ruman, Vlach, Volokh, Voloch, de l'autre; voir Encyclopaedia Britannica 1962).

"Les sources anciennes — dit l'auteur — indiquent le territoire habité par les Géto-Daces comme étant entouré par les Montagnes Slovaques, les Carpates du Nord, le Danube moyen et inférieur, la côte occidentale de la Mer Noire et la rivière Dniestr. Cette vaste étendue géographique doit être considérée comme autochtone car la formation des Géto-Daces en tant que peuple a eu lieu cette zone. Cependant à différentes périodes, des Scythes, Illyriens, Thraces, Celtes, Bastarnes, Sarmates se sont également établis sur le territoire de la Dacie. Les Gètes étaient le même peuple que les Daces et l'apogée de leur civilisation se situe au Ier siècle av. J.-C. et au Ier siècle de notre ère. Cette civilisation est caractérisée au point de vue matériel par le développement de la métallurgie du fer et le travail de celui-ci, par les débuts d'une architecture utilisant la pierre, surtout dans des buts militaires et religieux; par la croissance de la production agricole et pat l'apparition de quelques centres semi-urbains. Au point de vue spirituel, cette période montre l'acquisition et l'usage plutôt restreint de l'écriture, une certaine connaissance scientifique des plantes médicinales. Enfin, au point de vue politique, l'Etat, sous le règne de Burebista (env. 80-44 av. J.-C.) et de Décébal (87-106 de notre ère) représentait un réel danger pour la domination de Rome au sud du Danube" (pp. 35-36).

"Au début du IIe siècle, ce territoire était habité par les Daces. D'un autre côté, la présence des 'Rumanians' est notée par le notaire Anonymus du roi Béla III de Hongrie (Anonymus écrit "Blakhs" comme il en sera question plus loin; note de J.C.). Entre ces deux dates (1), séparées de huit siècles — 271-1050 environ —, un phénomène de la plus haute importance s'est produit: la transformation du peuple dace en un nouveau peuple, le peuple roumain ('Rumanian'). Linguistiquement, ce phénomène signifiait la disparition de la langue dace, du type 'satem', indo-européenne, et son remplacement par la langue roumaine, une langue 'Romance', dérivée du latin, du type 'kentum'. Ce changement et son aboutissement ne peuvent être expliqués que par le phénomène de la latinisation" (pp. 36-37) (2). Les anciennes langues indo-européennes se divisent en deux groupes selon que les sons "k" et "g" changent lorsqu'ils précèdent les voyelles "e" et "i". (Le groupe 'kentum' est ainsi nommé d'après le mot latin "kentum": cent; note de J.C.).

3. "La latinisation — continue l'auteur — est avant tout un phénomène linguistique, et en deuxieme lieu un phénomène spirituel. *Ce qui est le plus décisif, en tout cas, est le fait linguistique sans lequel la latinisation est inconcevable* (p. 37). Une population romanisée doit parler le latin, peu importe le caractère populaire, rustique, voire incorrect, non grammatical de ce dialecte, et doit avoir acquis la mentalité romaine ('forma mentis'), en adoptant les croyances, avec d'autres éléments de la culture spirituelle et matérielle des Romains. Si une population avec une culture du type provincial romain, parlant le latin, est mentionnée, et renonce dans certaines conditions historiques à ériger des inscriptions, et cesse ainsi de laisser à la postérité des preuves directes de sa langue, mais si elle continue de vivre dans ses agglomérations d'antan, d'utiliser les mêmes ustensiles, vases, ornements, etc., et d'enterrer ses morts selon les rites et rituels traditionnels, en même temps que ses agglomérations sont dépourvues d'éléments de culture matérielle indiquant la pénétration d'une population étrangère, il est entièrement correct d'en déduire qu'elle persiste dans la latinophonie" (p. 37).

4. L'auteur poursuit son étude avec les arguments qui doivent, selon lui, prouver le fait que les Daces n'ont pas été exterminés ni déplacés ou bannis par les conquérants romains. "Il y a plus de cent places aujourd'hui sur le territoire de la province romaine de Dacie (qui englobait non seulement la Transylvanie actuelle, mais une bonne partie de la Valachie, au sud des Carpates; note de J.C.) où les vestiges ont été identifiés comme appartenant à la population autochtone de l'époque de la domination romaine. Des diplômes militaires font mention de 13 à 15 unités auxiliaires formées de Daces. Les inscriptions latines de la Dacie contiennent environ deux pour cent de noms dont l'origine doit être thraco-dace, et une partie importante de ces deux pour cent appartient à la population locale. Des fragments de vases daces, faits à la main, poreux et peu cuits ont été trouvés dans certaines fouilles. Comme la présence des Daces est prouvée par l'archéologie (voir "fragments, etc." plus haut), par leurs agglomérations, cimetières, la présomption que tous les Thraco-Daces représentés par les inscriptions seraient des colons venus de l'autre côté (sud) du Danube, et que les troupes auxiliaires n'étaient pas recrutées parmi les Daces n'a pas de chance de survie"—conclut l'auteur (pp. 38-40).

5. "Deux conditions fondamentales devaient être réalisées —continue l'auteur—afin que les aspects territorial et démographique du déroulement de la romanisation puissent être compris. La première était la colonisation intense qui devait englober toute la province conquise par Rome, sans restriction aux centres urbains, mais couvrant aussi les régions rurales. La deuxième était la présence réelle de l'élément autochtone dace à côté des colons venus de l'Empire Romain. Eutropius, auteur antique (IVe siècle de notre ère) mentionne *infinitae copiae hominum ex tot orbe Romano*" venues en Dacie (3). Des trouvailles archéologiques et épigraphiques témoignent du caractère romain occidental de la colonisation. L'évidence en est fournie par environ 3.000 inscriptions latines découvertes en Dacie. Dans la sphère de la religion, la croyance en des dieux orientaux n'indique pas la répugnance envers la romanisation. De toute façon, le nombre relativement élevé des dieux orientaux ne constitue pas en soi une négation de la romanisation" (pp. 40-41).

6. "Le rôle des villes dans le processus de romanisation est unanimement reconnu". Il y avait, selon l'auteur, 12 villes — ou seulement 11 si on ne compte pas la ville de Malva qui n'est pas encore localisée —, dont sept étaient concentrées dans la région minière de Bihar. Les vestiges architecturaux existants de ces villes dénotent un caractère romain, et l'auteur conclut: "Comme nous venons de l'exposer, la continuité dace a été entièrement démontrée" (p. 44).

7. "La majorité de la population dace vivait naturellement à la campagne. Des vestiges appartenant à la population autochtone ont été trouvés dans les villes romaines, à Potaissa et à Napoca, mais leur nombre est maigre comparé aux découvertes dans les régions rurales. Le caractère rustique des agglomérations autochtones, le fait qu'elles contenaient la plus grande partie de la population dace ne signifie pas que le rôle des villes dans le processus de la romanisation n'a pas été important. La vie urbaine intense, même fastueuse, du type romain exerçait une forte influence sur les zones rurales avoisinantes. Comme le contact des colons avec la population locale était réalisé à la campagne, le rôle principal dans la romanisation était joué par les colons agricoles. Ces colons sont arrivés en Dacie par la voie officielle; quelques-uns probablement de leur propre initiative, mais la masse devait d'abord s'engager au service militaire. Environ 20 diplômes militaires ont été trouvés sur le territoire de la Dacie. Ceux-ci témoignent du grand nombre d'anciens combattants qui se sont établis définitivement en Dacie. L'établissement de ces anciens soldats s'est effectué naturellement dans les régions de leur service actif, et leur relation ainsi constituée avec la population locale attribuait un caractère de permanence à la romanisation. Agissant ensemble, tous ces facteurs de romanisation conduisirent à l'assimilation de la population autochtone sur une grande échelle" (pp. 46-47).

8. "Comme la romanisation est d'abord et en premier lieu un phénomène linguistique, il est évidemment plus difficile d'en définir les signes réels *en s'appuyant seulement sur l'archéologie* (4). Comparant des données linguistiques épigraphiques et archéologiques, il est possible d'arriver à *certaines* conclusions. On peut discuter concernant le nombre exact des mots daces reçus dans le latin populaire. Suivant des

estimations, celui-ci oscillerait entre 60 et 160 (5). Depuis longtemps, on reconnaît qu'environ deux pour cent des noms de personnes parmi les inscriptions latines en Dacie sont thraco-daces. Quelques-uns sont définitivement daces; d'autres peuvent ëtre également daces ou thraces, mais ils ne sont plus attribués exclusivement aux Thraces, maintenant que la continuité dace sous la domination de Rome — de 106 à 271 de notre ère — a été démontrée *par l'archéologie*. Le nombre relativement restreint de ces noms s'explique facilement: les autochtones, suffisamment romanisés pour laisser des inscriptions en latin, avaient le plus souvent abandonné leurs anciens noms pour adopter des noms romains (6). A présent que la continuité dace sous la domination romaine a été entièrement démontrée, *l'absence de vestiges de cultes autochtones* à l'époque romaine ne peut être interprétée autrement que par la romanisation relativement rapide. Le fait que la civilisation dace au temps de la domination romaine est représentée presque exclusivement par des éléments modestes: huttes, poterie faite a la main, tombes avec un inventaire relativement pauvre, peut ëtre la conséquence de la romanisation rapide de l'aristocratie autochtone, empressée de se concilier les bonnes grâces des vainqueurs romains pour préserver ses privilèges socio-économiques. Le fait que ce niveau d'assimilation a été atteint presque un demi-siècle avant 271 (vers environ 220 de notre ère-note de J.C.) ne doit surprendre personne" — dit l'auteur (pp. 47-49).

9. "En plus des territoires au nord du Danube, Rome régnait sur une autre vieille province, la Dobroudja, située entre la cours inférieur du Danube et la Mer Noire. Faisant partie de la province romaine de Moesia Inferior, cette région a subi une colonisation où l'élément thrace et oriental jouait un plus grand rôle qu'en Dacie. La Dobroudja présente un caractère gréco-romain: sa colonisation avec des éléments latinophones est quelque peu plus faible, mais cela est compensé par une durée plus longue: la Dobroudja fera partie de l'Empire Romain, et ensuite Romain-Byzantin jusqu'au VIIe siècle" (pp. 49-50, en tout 22 lignes).

10. "Dans les conditions historiques de la Dacie abandonnée par les Romains, en 271 de notre ère, où l'économie est probablement retombée à son état d'avant la conquete

romaine en 106, donc à l'état exclusivement rural, où les centres urbains tombaient en décadence, on ne devait pas être surpris de l'absence de monuments épigraphiques. Néanmoins de tels témoignages ne font pas entièrement défaut: l'anneau d'argent de Micia porte l'inscription *"Quartine vivas"*, et l'inscription sur un objet votif *"Ego Zenovius votum posui"*, ces deux objets datant du IVe siècle, *ne laissent aucun doute quant à la langue parlée* par ceux qui restaient dans la province après le départ des Romains" (p. 51).

11. "D'après les découvertes archéologiques, la deuxième moitié du Ve siècle s'ouvre sur une période de grands bouleversements et changements sur le territoire de la Dacie. La plupart des agglomérations, grandes et petites, connues comme ayant une population dace, ont l'air d'être abandonnées. Sans doute la raison doit en être recherchée dans la situation créée par l'effondrement de l'empire des Huns, suivant la mort d'Attila en 453, lorsque le territoire de l'ancienne Dacie romaine fut envahi par plusieurs peuples 'barbares' disputant leur suprématie sur l'héritage des Huns: une situation qui a forcé la population locale à chercher refuge en des endroits plus abrités. Bien que dans ces circonstances *la présence de la population autochtone ne se manifeste pas clairement par des trouvailles archéologiques,* de telles trouvailles ne manquent pas entièrement. En Transylvanie, par exemple, de telles agglomérations ont été trouvées à côté des cimetières des Gépides, un phénomène tout à fait inhabituel. *Nous tendons à penser* — ainsi s'exprime l'auteur — que ces agglomérations appartiennent à la population autochtone qui cohabitait avec les Gépides et empruntait un certain nombre d'éléments à leur culture matérielle" (p. 51).

12. "Tout cela montre — continue l'auteur — qu'on ne peut pas parler de l'abandon de la Dacie par la population dace (7). On peut pourtant dire avec assurance que certains déplacements de la population autochtone à l'intérieur de la Dacie ont eu lieu. Ce qui s'est passé a été la désertion des vieilles localités qui étaient sur le chemin des intrus, et la retraite vers les vallées, montagnes isolées, vers des endroits plus abrités des incursions des tribus migratoires. C'est le seul moyen d'expliquer *le fait que les noms des anciennes villes ont été oubliés et qu'elles ont reçu des noms slaves donnés par les Slaves.* Nous

savons maintenant que les noms slaves sont trouvés dans la plupart des cas dans les agglomérations situées sur la plaine ou dans les vallées ouvertes. C'est seulement après un certain laps de temps, assez court du reste, que la population autochtone est revenue à ces places ouvertes, pour se mêler aux Slaves qui seront graduellement assimilés" (p. 52).

13. "Parallèlement, mais non pas nécessairement en même temps, à la romanisation continue et profonde sur le territoire de la Dacie, une expansion de cette population et culture romanisée a eu lieu de la Dacie vers les régions qui n'étaient pas sous la dénomination directe de Rome. La disparition de la frontière romaine sur la ligne des Carpates a permis le déplacement vers ces régions de certains éléments de la Dacie. Il ne peut pas y avoir de doute que les *bergers avec leurs troupeaux* ont été les premiers à utiliser cet avantage d'une frontière non gardée pour se déplacer à leur gré à travers les montagnes" (p. 53).

* * *

14. Les points précédents présentent, en suivant l'auteur, Hadrian Daicoviciu, la théorie de la continuité daco-roumaine dont le but est de démontrer que la Transylvanie est le berceau de l'actuel peuple roumain. Son hypothèse fondamentale se trouve dans le point 2: les Daces étaient nombreux sous la domination de l'Empire Romain, de 106 à 271; Anonymus parle de Blakhs en 1200 environ (Anonymus n'écrit pas "Rumanians"—voir point 19); par conséquent les Blakhs d'Anonymus sont les Daces devenus Latins par leur langue, leur culture spirituelle et matérielle, et "ce changement et son aboutissement ne peuvent être expliqués que par le phénomène de leur romanisation".

Les Thraces étaient très nombreux, selon Hérodote, et les Géto-Daces formaient le groupe le plus important selon l'auteur; mais il nous apprend que déjà avant 106 d'autres peuples, tels les Scythes, Sarmates, etc. se sont aussi établis sur le territoire dace. Il est regrettable que parmi les 11 cartes du volume il n'y en ait pas une seule pour localiser "les plus de cent places" prouvant la présence des Daces en Transylvanie à l'époque romaine. Les trois mille inscription romaines prouvent la présence de l'Empire Romain, mais si la présence de l'Empire était une preuve d'une latinisation aussi rapide et aussi complète, en 165 ans entre 106 et 271, alors d'autres conquêtes romaines en Asie et en Afrique, aux Balkans, en Pannonie, etc. devraient présenter au moins le même degré de latinisation. La Dobroudja était un territoire géto-dace selon l'auteur. Elle était infiniment plus longtemps sous domination romaine et pourtant la Dobroudja ne présente aucune preuve de latinisation.

En ce qui concerne les objets que l'archéologie peut offrir comme preuve, l'auteur avoue qu'ils sont modestes: huttes, poterie, tombes avec un intentaire relativement pauvre, et cela peut être, suppose l'auteur, "la conséquence de la romanisation rapide de l'aristocratie autochtone, empressée de se concilier les bonnes grâces des vainqueurs romains" (point 8). Mais d'autres auteurs du volume, ainsi K. Horedt et M. Rusu, signalent dans leurs études que l'origine ethnique des objets archéologiques des VI-IXes siècles ne peut être établie — siècles pourtant très importants pour la continuité supposée des Daces. Pour un autre auteur, Dan Gh. Teodor, ces objets ne fournissent que des indications socio-économiques.

Il faut aussi ajouter que l'auteur mentionne des régions montagneuses, hautes vallées abritées où la population dace aurait cherché refuge devant les invasions "barbares". Par contre, K. Horedt et M. Rusu déclarent que les Daces sont restés dans leurs villages ancestraux. Ion Donat, autre auteur du volume, croit avoir trouvé les preuves de la survivance des Daces dans les vallées méridionales des Carpates, donc pas en Transylvanie. Ce territoire est connu dans l'histoire hongroise sous le nom de UNGROVLACHIA, au XIIIe siècle.

Il est enfin intéressant de noter que selon les historiens roumains, Décébal était un roi puissant qui pouvait mobiliser 200.000 soldats et que l'écriture était connue parmi les Daces de son temps. Pourtant aucune réapparition d'un quelconque Etat dace après le départ des Romains en 271 n'est connue et aucune trace du culte religieux des Daces ne subsiste de l'époque de la domination romaine, selon l'auteur. "La plus ancienne source écrite — dit S. Olteanu, autre auteur du volume — de l'existence de quelques formations politiques sur le territoire actuel de la Roumanie (en Transylvanie et dans la région de la rivière Temes; note de J.C.) est la GESTA HUN-GARORUM du notaire royal Anonymus" déjà plusieurs fois cité (p. 251).

15. "La latinisation est avant tout un phénomène linguisti-que — dit H. Daicoviciu. Ce qui est le plus décisif en tout cas, est le fait linguistique sans lequel la latinisation est inconcevable" (point 3). Mais nous lisons immédiatement après dans le point 3 qu'il n'y a pas de preuves linguistiques du tout, sauf six mots latins pour 929 ans de continuité — daco-roumaine hypothétique — de 271 jusqu'à Anonymus en 1200: un anneau d'argent portant l'inscription "QUARTINE VIVAS" et un objet votif avec quatre mots "EGO ZENOVIUS VOTUM POSUI". Six mots ne peuvent rien prouver pour une période de neuf siècles et un quart.

En ce qui concerne la langue dace, le linguiste Al. Graur, un des auteurs du volume, avoue qu'il n'existe aucune preuve écrite de la langue dace ou d'autres langues thraces. Il mentionne l'existence d'environ 80 mots d'origine *albanaise* dans l'actuelle langue roumaine. H. Daicoviciu, par contre, indique 60 a 160 mots *"daces* reçus dans le latin populaire" — ce latin populaire étant par conséquent la base du Roumain actuel, mais qui n'est pas le latin classique de l'époque de la domination romaine entre 106 et 271. Quant à la langue albanaise, Al. Graur écrit qu'on la considère comme la continuation de la langue illyrienne, "mais nous ignorons, dit-il, les relations exactes entre la langue thrace et illyrienne" (p. 317 du volume). Ces mots albanais représentent d'importantes notions de géographie et de biologie et indiquent par conséquent un voisinage prolongé des Albanais et des Roumains. Ce fait désigne les régions centrales des Balkans comme l'habitat originaire des Roumains — et surtout pas un territoire au nord du Danube. Cela est corroboré par d'autres faits amplement prouvés.

Il faut souligner encore que, selon l'auteur, la langue dace, par ailleurs inconnue, n'appartient pas aux dialectes thraces; par contre, Al. Graur la considère comme une branche de ces dialectes. Selon l'opinion généralement acceptée, l'histoire d'une langue fournit des explications valables quant à l'origine ethnique d'un peuple. On peut constater que les adeptes de la théorie de la continuité daco-roumaine ne disposent de preuves linguistiques ni pour la latinisation des Daces ni pour la langue dace elle-même.

Il faut encore mentionner ici les soi-disant "Daces libres": les Daces qui, selon l'auteur, vivaient en dehors des limites de la Dacie occupée par l'Empire Romain. C'est un territoire considérable comprenant la Dobroudja et l'espace entre le Danube inférieur, la Mer Noire, la rivière Dniestr et la chaîne des Carpates. Il est parfaitement justifié de poser la question: comment ces "Daces libres"—donc non assujettis à Rome et a son influence latine—sont-ils devenus "Roumains"? L'auteur croit trouver la réponse dans le déplacement périodique des "bergers avec leurs troupeaux" répandant la langue et la culture latine dans ces régions non occupées. Est-il possible de croire à l'efficacité d'une méthode d'assimilation pareille? Est-il possible que ces "Daces libres" n'auraient rien conservé de leur langue dace?

16. Le rôle des villes dans la romanisation peut être très important. Mais, selon l'auteur, "la majorité des Daces vivaient, naturellement, à la campagne. Le nombre des vestiges appartenant à la population dace dans les villes de Potaissa et de Napoca—l'auteur mentionne seulement ces deux villes—est maigre." La latinisation supposée des Daces devait s'accomplir par conséquent, à la campagne. Pour preuve, l'auteur suggère qu'il y avait de nombreux Daces et de nombreux colons: "infinitae copiae hominum ex toto orbe Romano" (8). Ces colons devaient d'abord servir dans les légions; mais, pense l'auteur, à la fin de leur service actif, ils sont restés sur place avec la population dace, et c'est ainsi que les Daces ont été latinisés, "si rapidement qu'un niveau très élevé a déjà été réalisé vers l'an 220, presque un demi-siècle avant la fin de la domination romaine (en 271)".

Tout cela montre clairement que les villes n'ont pas joué un role important dans la latinisation supposée; d'autant moins que sur les 11 villes romaines connues sur le territoire de la Dacie, 7 étaient concentrées sur une région restreinte des montagnes de Bihar. De toute façon, le nombre des villes était trop faible pour opérer une telle latinisation, surtout au cours d'une période si courte: 165 ans en tout. En outre, le fait est bien connu que les colons, ces "infinitae copiae hominum" venaient de tous les coins de l'Empire Romain; dans leur majorité ils n'étaient pas de langue maternelle latine, et le plus souvent ils séjournaient dans la province, sans s'y établir d'une façon permanente. Dans ces conditions, l'efficacité de leur influence quant à la latinisation des Daces est plutôt douteuse.

17. Les "conclusions" que l'auteur croit pouvoir tirer des données archéologiques sont les suivantes:

a) on peut discuter concernant le nombre exact des mots daces (selon Al. Graur, mots albanais, environ 80) reçus dans le latin populaire; selon des estimations il serait de 60 à 160 selon l'auteur;

b) parmi les inscriptions latines de l'époque romaine en Dacie, environ deux pour cent de noms de personnes sont thraco-daces; quelques-uns sont définitivement daces;

c) des éléments archéologiques presque exclusivement modestes: huttes, poterie, tombes avec un inventaire relativement pauvre, datant de l'époque de la domination de l'Empire Romain (point 8).

Les quelques noms supposés daces parmi environ deux pour cent de noms thraco-daces, trouvés dans les trois mille inscriptions latines léguées par la domination romaine, ne semblent pas présenter une preuve suffisante, avec ou sans les objets archéologiques, d'un grand nombre de Daces au temps de la domination de Rome, ni de leur latinisation complète ou incomplète, ni de leur survivance jusqu'au temps d'Anonymus.

18. Par contre, l'histoire connait les grands bouleversements des peuples au cours du premier millénaire de notre ère. Les Goths étaient en Transylvanie depuis l'an 300 (9) et les Huns y ont aussi fait leur apparition. Après la mort d'Attila, en 453, les Gépides étaient les maîtres du bassin des Carpates depuis le Danube moyen jusqu'aux Carpates de l'Est. Vers le milieu du VIe siècle, les Avars ont pris la place des Gépides, et avec des tribus slaves à leur service ils ont plusieurs fois dévasté la Transylvanie et les Balkans jusqu'aux murs de Constantinople. Arnold Tonynbee, dans son livre CONSTANTINE PORPHYROGENITUS AND HIS WORLD (London, 1973) dit, citant John of Ephesus (p. 633): "Les années 581-2 ont vu l'invasion d'un peuple maudit, appelé les Slaves qui ont envahi toute la Grèce, le pays des Thessaloniens et toute la Thrace; ils ont occupé les villes et de nombreuses forteresses, ont dévasté

et brûlé, ont réduit la population a l'esclavage . . .". A. Toyn-bee ajoute que l'Empire Byzantin a été envahi par 100.000 Slaves dans ces mêmes années 581-2.

A la suite de ces bouleversements, "la plupart des agglo-mérations grandes et petites, connues pour avoir abrité une population dace, ont l'air d'avoir été abandonnées", dit l'auteur (point 11). La population locale a été contrainte de se réfugier en des endroits plus abrités: vers les vallées et montagnes isolées. Mais nous avons vu dans le point 2 que, selon l'auteur, la population autochtone, dace, restait dans ses agglomérations, qu'elle ne se mélangeait pas avec les envahis-seurs gépides, huns, avars, etc.

D'un autre côté, l'auteur déclare, selon le point 11, que des cimetières communs de Gépides et d'autochtones ont été trouvés en Transylvanie. "Nous tendons à penser, dit l'auteur, que les Gépides et les autochtones vivaient ensemble et que ces derniers ont emprunté un certain nombre d'éléments" à la culture matérielle des Gépides. Tout cela invalide l'affir-mation précédente selon laquelle les autochtones, supposés daces, ne se sont pas mélangés avec les envahisseurs, et qu'il n'y a pas eu de pénétration de culture matérielle étrangère chez eux. Un peu plus loin l'auteur reconnait qu'à la suite des in-vasions "les noms des anciennes villes ont été oubliés et ces villes ont reçu des noms slaves, donnés par des Slaves" (point 12).

Tout cela est en contradiction avec les affirmations déjà citées de l'auteur. Nous avons déjà mentionné que les objets archéologiques seuls, par eux-mêmes, ne sont pas suffisants pour prouver leur origine ethnique, c'est-à-dire l'existence de tel ou tel peuple qui les aurait produits. Les auteurs M. Rusu et C. Preda du volume en question considèrent impossible l'identification des peuples de la "Völkerwanderung" sur la base d'objets archéologiques. K. Horedt (p. 113-4 du livre) et M. Rusu (p. 135 ibid.) deux auteurs déja cités du volume, déclarent qu'il n'y a pas de traces d'agglomérations et de noms géographiques daces dans les "montagnes et vallées abritées" où H. Daicoviciu les place, après avoir quitté leurs villages pour chercher refuge devant les envahisseurs.

19. Anonymus mentionne le mot "blakh" dans les parties 24, 25, 26 et 44 de son livre: "Tuhutum (Tétény, Töhötöm) a

pris connaissance de la bonne qualité de la terre au-delà de la forêt ('terra ultra silvana', Transylvanie, Erdély) où un certain Blakh Gelou (Gyalu) régnait "sur des Blakhs et Slovènes" (partie 24). "Lorsqu'ils (les Hongrois) voulaient passer par la rivière Temes, le maître de cette région, Glad (Galad), s'est opposé à eux à la tête d'une grande armée de cavalerie et d'infanterie, et en outre avec une aide coumane, bulgare et blakh" (partie 44).

Anonymus a écrit l'histoire de la conquête hongroise du bassin des Carpates trois siècles après les événements. Même si on suppose qu'il disposait d'une description précédente (GESTA UNGARORUM, du temps du roi Ladislas I, 1077-1095), il ne possédait aucun témoignage direct de la conquête. Il n'y a pas de doute qu'il a inventé des noms, a créé des princes (dux) pour placer en face des conquérants magyars des adversaires dignes d'être conquis. Il est tres significatif que des personnages historiques importants de la deuxieme moitié du IXe siècle — époque de la conquete magyare — Anonymus n'en mentionne aucun, ainsi les deux Svatopluk, princes de Moravie, Arnulf, empereur, allemand, Siméon, tsar bulgare, ne sont pas du tout mentionnés. Par contre, Anonymus fait descendre les Hongrois de Magog, fils de Japhet, personnage biblique, et parle des Coumans dans l'armée de Glad, avant l'an 907, bien que les Coumans ne soient apparus que vers 1050 dans les steppes de la Russie, venant de l'Asie.

Les "Slovènes" mentionnés par Anonymus disent eux-mêmes dans le texte comment "le Grand Khan, l'ancêtre du prince Salan, qui est venu de la Bulgarie suivant le conseil de l'Empereur des Grecs, et avec son aide, a occupé ce territoire" (gardé par ces Slovènes). Ils disent encore qu'ils venaient eux-mêmes de la Bulgarie. Ainsi ces Slovènes apparaissent comme étant des Slavs au service et sous les ordres des Bulgares. La figure légendaire de Menumorout dans les Montagnes de Bihar parle aussi "de mon maître l'Empereur de Constantinople"; Salan, le grand adversaire des Hongrois, était sans aucun doute un Bulgare. A l'époque de la conquête magyare, la Transylvanie était une possession bulgare et c'est ce fait qui est prouvé par Anonymus, et par les noms géographiques de cette région.

20. Quant aux Vlachs ou Blakhs chez Anonymus, les tribus thraco-illyriennes dans les Balkans, étaient originairement désignés par ce nom. Plus tard, à la suite de leur descente dans les Balkans, les Slaves ont employé ce nom pour désigner les habitants de la Macédoine, appelée GRANDE VALACHIE, descendants des habitants néo-latins de ces régions. C'est ici que ces bergers nomades sont devenus chrétiens de rite slave de Cyrille et Méthode et placés sous l'autorité de l'archevêque bulgare d'Ochrida.

Les auteurs grecs de Byzance, les mieux renseignés car les plus intéressés aux peuples qui entouraient et menaçaient l'Empire Byzantin, parlent fréquemment des Bulgares et aussi des Hongrois, pourtant les contacts de ces derniers avec Byzance étaient sporadiques et lointains. Mais ces auteurs ne savent absolument rien de Vlachs ou "Roumains" ou Daces en Transylvanie ou au sud des Carpates.

Arnold Toynbee, dans son livre cité, déclare que les peuples habitant les Balkans et parlant le latin ont été décimés par les Slaves et les Avars. Néanmoins, selon lui, ces Néo-latins n'étaient pas entièrement exterminés, mais sont devenus des partenaires des Bulgares slavisés dans l'Etat bulgaro-vlach lorsque ces deux peuples ont uni leurs forces en 1185-7 pour se libérer du joug de l'empereur de Byzance. Ainsi les Vlachs et les Bulgares, sous la conduite des frères Ivan et Peter Asen, ont reconquis l'indépendance de la Bulgarie et Ivan a pris le titre de "tsar" des Bulgares et des Grecs (p. 562). "Bien que la langue roumaine actuelle — continue A. Toynbee — soit une langue 'Romance', le Slave de la Macédoine de Cyrille et de Méthode a été la langue administrative et liturgique de la Valachie et de la Moldavie encore au XIVe siècle, et est demeurée la langue liturgique jusqu'en 1679. La Bible a été traduite en Roumain en 1688 en Transylvanie hongroise" (A. Toynbee, *op. cit.*, 523).

Finalement, dans une note de la page 457, nous lisons encore ceci dans le livre d'Arnold Toynbee: "L'évidence archéologique montre que la Valachie était peuplée *jusqu'à la fin du Xe siècle* par une population sédentaire que Petre Diaconu (coéditeur et auteur du volume en question) affirme être de langue roumaine. Au temps de Constantin Porphyrogénete (905-959), selon le livre de ce dernier: DE ADMINIST-

RANDO IMPERIO (10), chapitre 42 — les Petchenègues et les Bulgares avaient une frontière commune, ce qui signifie que la Valachie à cette époque-là était territoire petchenègue. Diaconu essaie de modifier l'affirmation de l'Empereur Constantin; son rejet d'une autorité bien informée du Xe siècle est arbitraire et suspect d'être influencé par des considérations politiques de nos jours". L'autorité d'Arnold Toynbee dispense de tout commentaire.

Ajoutons encore que le chroniqueur de Kiev, au milieu du XIe siècle, parlant du passage des Hongrois près de Kiev à la fin du IXe siecle, appelle les Carpates "Montagnes des Ougors" — Montagnes Hongroises, au lieu de les appeler Montagnes Daces ou Vlachs ou même "Roumaines". Les noms géographiques de la Roumanie prouvent aussi les changements des peuples sur ce territoire: noms hongrois, turcs, iraniens, slaves.

L'histoire de ce territoire n'est pas identique à l'histoire du peuple appelé aujourd'hui roumain. Ce n'est pas la continuité que les faits prouvent mais des changements des populations. Les Daces et les Roumains d'aujourd'hui sont deux ethnies différentes. (*Documentation sur l'Europe Centrale*, Vol. XVIII, No. 2, 1979)

NOTES

(1) La date de l'an 1050 environ représente pour les adeptes de la continuité daco-roumaine le début de la lente pénétration — selon eux — des Hongrois en Transylvanie.

(2) Les auteurs du livre emploient "romanisation" et "latinophonie". Les deux termes désignent au fond le même phénomène: la transformation linguistique et culturelle des Daces. La "latinisation" indique cette transformation selon la théorie de la continuité daco-roumaine.

(3) Auteur du "*Breviarium ab urbe condita*" de la fondation de la ville de Rome jusqu'à l'accession de l'Empereur Valens, en 364. Son oeuvre est caractérisée par l'impartialité et par une grande précision.

(4) L'influence de la culture matérielle romaine est manifeste à travers les anciennes provinces et territoires limitrophes de l'Empire Romain, sans que les habitants de ces territoires deviennent pour autant "Romains" de culture spirituelle et matérielle.

(5) André Du Nay, dans son livre remarquable: *The Early History of the Rumanian Language* (Jupiter Press, Lake Bluff, Illinois, USA, 1977, 275 pages) donne une analyse exhaustive et précise de ce problème. Ouvrage indispensable par sa richesse et par sa précision objective, pour la connaissance de la théorie de la continuité daco-roumaine.

(6) Plusieurs révoltes des Daces contre les conquérants romains laissent pourtant supposer que leur latinisation n'était ni rapide ni profonde.

(7) Eutropius écrit concernant la retraite romaine: ". . . *abductosque Romanos ex urbibus et agris Daciae, in media Moesia collocavit* . . .". Les Romains ont créé deux

provinces au sud du Danube à l'occasion de leur retraite: Dacia Ripensis et Dacia Mediterranea, et ont établi la population évacuée dans ces provinces.

(8) Voir A. Du Nay (*op. cit.*, pp. 178 et 180): "After the (Roman) conquest, the new colony (Dacia) was populated by people coming from the whole Roman world, probably from 20 provinces".

"During the third century, the number of Oriental elements in the population increased. Many non-latin people, mostly from the Near-East, had their own organisations, according to their nationality or religion."

(9) Les Goths ont attaqué l'Empire Romain déjà vers 213-14 de notre ère.

(10) Voir A. Toybee (*op. cit.*, pp. 5 et 16): "De Administrando Imperio appears to have been written between A.D. 948 and perhaps 952. . . . Constantine was a natural-born scholar."

The most recent version of the theory of Daco-Rumanian continuity

Summary

The author's discussion is centered on a chapter in the recently published book, *Relations between the Autotochthonous Population and the Migratory Populations on the territory of Rumania* (Bucharest, Academy of Social and Political Sciences of the Socialist Republic of Rumania, 1975) edited by Miron Constantinescu, Stefan Pascu and Petre Diaconu. Of the twenty-one studies written by Rumanian specialists, Jean Csonka has chosen for his discussion Hadrian Daicoviciu's contribution entitled "Dacians and Romans in the Province of Trajan."

Daicoviciu's goal is to show that Transylvania is the birthplace of the Rumanian nation. His hypothesis is that Dacians were very numerous in the area when it was under the domination of the Roman Empire from 106 to 271 A.D. The presence of "Rumanians" is noted by Anonymus, the notary of King Béla III of Hungary (1172-90). Actually, however, Anonymus writes about Blakhs, not Rumanians around 1200. Daicoviciu, however, claims that the Blakhs Anonymus mentions are identical with the Dacian ancestors of the Rumanians. During the period of Roman occupation, Daicovicius claims that a rapid Latinization of the Dacian language and culture took place and that the Dacians became Rumanians. There are several problems with this theory. There is no proof that the Dacians were the only group living in the area at the time. Herodotos says that the Thracians are a very large group, but Daicoviciu claims that the Geto-Dacians formed the largest group of Thracians, and that before 106, Scythians, Sarmatians, etc. already inhabited Transylvania. Archeological evidence to that effect is negligible; few objects have been found in the area which can be clearly called Dacian. The ethnic origin of archeological objects from the 4th to 9th centuries cannot be established. Daicoviciu claims that the scarcity of autochthonous objects is evidence of a rapid and complete Latinization. This does not explain, however, why Roman conquests in other similar areas such as the Balkans, Asia, Africa, etc. have not shown the same degree of Latinization. Daicoviciu also maintains that the Dacian population sought refuge from the "barbaric" invasions in the mountainous regions. On the other hand, K. Horedt and M. Rusu, in their respective studies included in the book, declair that the Dacians stayed in their ancestral villages, while Ion Donat, another author of the volume, believes he found proof that the Dacians survived that period outside Transylvania, in the valleys of the Carpathians.

Latinization, according to Daicoviciu, is primarily a linguistic phenomenon. But we read elsewhere in the book that linguistic proof is applicable only to 6 Latin words for 929 years of continuity. Al. Graur, a linguist, and another author of the book, admits that there is not one written proof of the Dacian or other Thracian languages. He speaks of about 80 words of Albanian origin in the Rumanians language. While Albanian is considered as the continuation of the Illyrian languages, we don't know the exact relations between the Thracian and Illyrian languages. Albanian words in the Rumanian certainly indicate that the Albanians and Rumanians were long-time neighbors and that the original habitat of the Rumanians is the central region of the Balkans, and not the territory north of the Danube.

Great upheavals had taken place during the first 1000 years of our era: Goths were in Transylvania since 300 A.D. followed by the Huns; after the death of Attila, in 453, the Gepids became the masters of the Carpathian Basin; in the middle of the 6th century the Avars took the place of the Gepids and with Slavic tribes in their service they devastated repeatedly Transylvania and the Balkans. In his book, "Constantine Porphyrogenitus and his world" Arnold Toynbee says that the Slavic devastated and burned down the towns and forttresses and reduced the population to slavery. He further says that although the present-day Rumanian is a "Romance" language, the Slav was still the administrative and liturgical language of Wallachia and Moldavia in the 14th century, and remained the liturgical language until as late as 1679. The Bible, Toynbee says, was translated into Rumanian in 1688 in Hungarian Transylvania. As Toynbee points out on page 457 of his book, archeological evidence shows that Wallachia was inhabited until the end of the 10th century by a stationary population which—according to Petre Diaconu (coeditor and author of the book here discussed)—spoke Rumanian. But in the time of Constantine Porphyrogenitus (905-959) the Pecheneggs and the Bulgars had common frontier which signifies that Wallachia was at that time a Pechenegg territory. Diaconu, Toynbee points out, attempted to modify Emperor Constantine's assertion; his rejection of a well informed authority of the 10th century is arbitrary and suspect of being influenced by present political considerations. Finally, it should be noted that the 11th century chronicler of Kiev, while reffering to the Hungarians near Kiev at the end of the 9th century, calls the Carpathians "Mountains of Ougors", Hungarian Mountains, instead of calling them Dacian or Vlach, let alone "Rumanian" Mountains. In general, the geographic names of Rumania, Hungarian, Turkish, Iranian, Slavic, attest to great population changes in this area. Thus this territory's history cannot be claimed exclusively as the history of the peoples called Rumanian today. The facts prove the changing of the populations rather, than the continuity of a single people. The ancient Dacians and the modern Rumanians are certainly two different ethnic groups.

DIE ALBANISCH-RUMÄNISCHE
WANDERUNGSBEWEGUNG
(11. – 13. JAHRHUNDERT)

This is the 13th chapter of the "History of Southeast Europe" ("Geschichte Südosteuropas") by *Georg Stadtmüller* published by *R. Oldenbourg* München Wien (1976).
This chapter is reprinted here with the permission of the publisher.

Die Volkstumskarte Südosteuropas wurde im Hoch- und
Spätmittelalter durch zwei grosse Siedlungsbewegungen völlig
umgestaltet: vom Westen her durch die deutsche Kolonisation,
die im Zuge der grossen abendländischen Ostbewegung ein-
drang, und gleichzeitig, aber in umgekehrter Richtung — vom
Südosten her — durch die albanisch-rumänische Siedlungsausbreitung.

Ein halbes Jahrtausend vorher hatte die awarisch-slawische
Landnahme (um 600) den geschlossenen Volkstumsblock der
Balkanromanen aufgesplittert. Die Massen der slawischen
Ackerbauern waren über die Donau herübergekommen und
hatten das offene Land besetzt. Die balkanromanische Bevölkerung wurde verdrängt. Ein Teil flüchtete nach den
befestigten Städten, vor allem in den Küstenstrichen längs des
Schwarzen und Adriatisch-Jonischen Meeres. Dort konnten sie
sich viele Jahrhunderte lang behaupten. Erst im Hoch- und
Spätmittelalter gewann dann das durch Unterwanderung
vordringende slawische Volkstum in den romanischen Städten
Dalmatiens die Vorherrschaft, während sich auf den vorgela-
gerten dalmatinischen Inseln das Romanentum noch länger
hielt.

Ein anderer Teil der alten balkanromanischen Bevölkerung bewahrte als Hirten in den Bergen Sprache und Volkstum. Dies waren die Vorfahren der heutigen Albaner und Rumänen. Beide Völker haben vom 7. bis 11. Jahrhundert als
schweifende Viehzüchter auf den Bergen gelebt ohne eine äus-
sere staatliche Geschichte. Erst seit der Jahrtausendwende
werden sie bei den byzantinischen Geschichtsschreibern über-
haupt erwähnt.

Über ihre innere Entwicklungsgeschichte während des dunklen halben Jahrtausends nach der slawischen Landnahme (600—1100) gibt die kulturgeschichtliche Ausdeutung des Sprachbestandes ("Wörter und Sachen") hinlänglichen Aufschluss. Beide Völker lebten nach Ausweis ihrer zahlreichen Sprachgemeinsamkeiten in einer engen, lange dauernden Symbiose. Die Heimat des uralbanischen und frühalbanischen Volkes lag in vorslawischer und nachslawischer Zeit in dem nordalbanischen Bergland. Demnach muss auch die Heimat der mit ihnen benachbarten rumänischen Hirtenstämme unweit davon gelegen haben.

Aus diesen Erkenntnissen lässt sich die Frühgeschichte der Albaner und Rumänen in ihren Hauptlinien zurückverfolgen: Die allgemeine Romanisierung hatte im Verlauf der römischen Kaiserzeit den gesamten inneren Balkan erfasst und umgestaltet. Von der adriatischen Küstenzone und von den grossen Garnisonen an der Donaugrenze aus wurde allmählich das ganze Binnenland romanisiert. Zunächst ging die Bevölkerung der Städte zum Gebrauch der lateinischen Reichssprache über, es folgten die Bauern des offenen Landes und schliesslich auch die Hirten der Berge. Die Stämme der Wanderhirten haben sich auf ihren Bergen am längsten der Romanisierung entzogen. Noch im 6. Jahrhundert wurde die thrazische Mundart der Bessen vereinzelt gesprochen. Im nordalbanischen Mati-Gau, durch schwer übersteigbare Gebirgswälle von der zersetzenden Berührung mit der römischen Reichskultur und der lateinischen Reichssprache geschützt, konnten die uralbanischen Hirten ihre angestammte Sprache noch behaupten. Aber dem übermächtigen Einfluss der Romanisierung wäre auch die Mundart der Uralbaner mit der Zeit erlegen. Schritt um Schritt drangen lateinische Elemente auch in das Uralbanische ein. Die Romanisierung war im standigen Vordringen. Hatte diese Entwicklung noch ein Jahrhundert angedauert, dann wären auch die Uralbaner zu Balkanromanen geworden. Nur die slawische Landnahme hat die Uralbaner vor dem Versinken im Meere des Balkanromanentums bewahrt. Der Einfluss der Romanisierung wurde durch das Eindringen der Slawen plötzlich unterbrochen. Die uralbanische Mundart, mitten in der Romanisierung begriffen, erstarrte auf jener Entwicklungsstufe, die sie unter der Einwirkung der Romanisierung zur Zeit der slawischen Landnahme erreicht hatte. (Das heutige Albanische besteht noch etwa zu einem Viertel aus lateinischen Lehnworten.)

Nach der slawischen Landnahme haben die Albaner und die stammverwandten Rumänen ("Wlachen") nahezu ein halbes Jahrtausend hindurch ein fast geschichtsloses Leben geführt. Während die fruchtbaren Ebenen und Hügellandschaften von slawischen Ackerbauern besetz waren, lebten die Wanderhirtenschwärme der Albaner und Rumänen in der Mattenregion der Hochgebirge, wo ihre Herden die besten Weidemöglichkeiten vorfanden. Zu Anbruch der kalten Jahreszeit gaben sie ihre Alm- und Sennereiwirtschaft auf den Bergen auf und zogen mit ihren Herden wieder talwärts, um in wärmeren Flusstälern oder in der Küstenebene zu überwintern.

So verlief die Geschichte dieser Wanderhirtenschwärme Jahrhunderte hindurch — Geschichte abseits der Weltgeschichte. Die Raubinstinkte dieser Hirtenstämme waren gebändigt durch das grossbulgarische Reich, in dessen Rahmen sie lebten. Solange das balkanische Binnenland unter bulgarischer Herrschaft zusammengefasst war, mussten auch die Albaner und Rumänen wohl oder übel Ruhe halten. Als aber dann zu Ende des 10. Jahrhunderts das grossbulgarische Reich unter den Schlägen der oströmischen Armeen auseinanderbrach, da war die geschichtliche Stunde der beiden Hirtenvölker gekommen. Nun treten sie zum ersten Male in der Mittagshelle der Geschichte hervor. Und es dauerte nur zwei kurze Jahrhunderte, da waren beide Völker bereits zu gewichtigen politischen Faktoren auf der Balkanhalbinsel geworden.

*

Die Albaner erscheinen im 11. Jahrhundert zum ersten Male in den Berichten zeitgenössischer Geschichtsschreiber — schon damals in jener Rolle, die sie seitdem fast ununterbrochen gespielt haben: als Söldner im Dienste fremder Herren. Schon bald darauf muss ihre grosse Siedlungsausbreitung eingesetzr haben. Die aufgestaute Volkstumskraft quoll über die Gebirgsränder des Mati-Gaues heraus. Im 11. und 12. Jahrhundert wurde das Küstenland Niederalbaniens, im 13. Jahrhundert Westmazedonien und Südalbanien besiedelt.

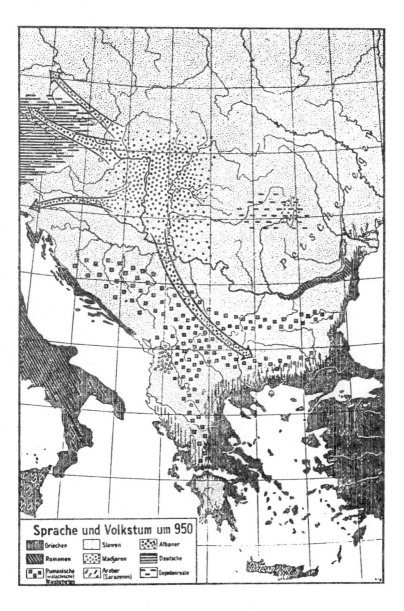

Sprache und Volkstum um 950

Griechen · Slawen · Albaner
Romanen · Madjaren · Deutsche
Rumänische (walachische) Wandertriften · Araber (Sarazenen) · Gepidenreste

Und als nach dem Tod des Serbenzaren Stephan IV. Duschan (1331 — 1355) das gross-serbische Reich auseinanderbrach, da setzte ein mächtiges Vordringen der Albaner auch nach Süden ein. Zunächst wurde Epirus besiedelt, dessen nördlicher und westlicher Teil (Südalbanien und Tschamerija) noch heute albanischer Volkstumsboden ist. Dann ging die albanische Ausbreitung weiter nach Akarnanien, Ätolien und von hier aus einerseits über den Golf von Korinth nach Morea hinüber, andererseits nach Böotien und Attika. Im Zuge der venezianischen Siedlungspolitik wurden dann sogar auf die Inselwelt des Ägäischen Meeres Albaner verpflanzt.

Rund die Hälfte des griechischen Volkstumsbodens wurde damals von den Albanern besetzt.In welchem zahlenmässigen Verhältnis griechische Altsiedler und albanishe Neusiedler zueinander standen, und wie sich das Zusammenleben der beiden Völker gestaltete, bleibt unklar. Im Laufe der Jahrhunderte hat dann das Griechentum durch seine kulturelle Überlegenheit und vor allem durch die kulturelle Wirksamkeit der orthodoxen Kirche das verlorene Gebiet Schritt für Schritt zurückgewonnen. Die orthodoxen Albaner nahmen unter kirchlichem Einfluss die griechische Sprache an und begannen bald, sich selbst als Griechen zu fühlen.

Die Albaner des Mutterlandes sind im 13. und 14. Jahrhundert stark unter den abendländischen Kultureinfluss geraten, der durch das angiovinische Königreich Neapel und die benachbarten venezianischen Besitzungen vermittelt wurde. Im 15. Jahrhundert wurden sie dann durch die anbrechende Türkenherrschaft zu einer erneuten Siedlungsausbreitung veranlasst. Die neue Auswanderung spielte sich in verschiedenen Formen ab: Zunächst verliessen grössere Massen Albaner als Flüchtlinge ihre Wohnsitze in Albanien und Morea und siedelten sich in Italien (Sizilien, Kalabrien, Basilicata, Apulien, Rosciano) an.

*

Die mit den Albanern sprachverwandten Rumänen haben eine grössere und reichere Geschichte. Im 10. Jahrhundert werden die "wlachischen"Wanderhirten zum ersten Male in der Gegend von Kastoria, also im Grenzgebiet Thessaliens und Mazedoniens erwähnt. Der mächtige Gebirgsstock des Pindus war schon damals von Rumänen besiedelt. Aber auch überall sonst,

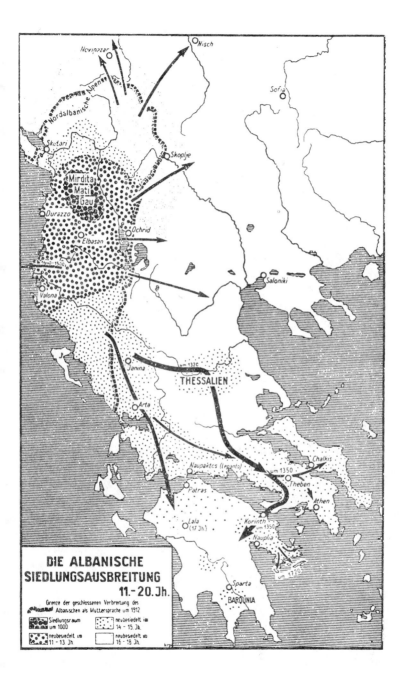

Novipazar

Nisch

Sofia

Nordalbanische Alpen

Skutari

Skoplje

Mirdita
Mati
Gau

Durazzo

Ochrid

Elbasan

Saloniki

Valona

Janina

um 1320

THESSALIEN

Arta

Naupaktos (Lepanto)

Chalkis

um 1350

Theben

Patras

Athen

Lala
(17.Jh.)

Korinth
um 1350

Nauplia

um 1770

**DIE ALBANISCHE
SIEDLUNGSAUSBREITUNG
11.- 20.Jh.**

Sparta

BARDUNIA

Grenze der geschlossenen Verbreitung des
Albanischen als Muttersprache um 1912

Siedlungsraum
um 1000

neubesiedelt im
14 - 15. Jh.

neubesiedelt im
11 - 13.Jh.

neubesiedelt im
16 - 18.Jh.

wo in der Hochregion der Berge günstige Weideplätze vorhanden waren, gab es rumanische Hirten. So in Mazedonien, Serbien, Bulgarien und in den Bergen Dalmatiens (Maurowlachen, d.h. "schwarze Wlachen", später "Morlakken" genannt). Daneben aber scheint es am Unterlauf der Donau damals sesshafte Romanen gegeben zu haben, die Nachkommen der balkanromanischen Bevölkerung der Donaustädte, die an der Kulturentwicklung des grossbulgarischen Reiches im Frühmittelalter einen bedeutenden Anteil gehabt hat. Nach der Eroberung dieses Gebietes durch die Oströmer (972) wurde es dem oströmischen Reich als Provinz *Paristrion* einverleibt. Dann tauchten um 1100 auf dem rechten Ufer der Donau — in der heutigen Dobrudscha — örtliche Kleinherrschaften auf, deren Führer turkvölkische (kumanische oder petschenegische) Namen targen. Die rumänische Bevölkerung wurde hier also von einer turkvölkischen Herrenschicht politisch organisiert.

Die grosse Ausbreitung des rumänischen Volkes in das damals noch unerschlossene Urwaldgebiet der Karpaten ging aber nicht von den sesshaften Romanen des Paristrion, sondern von den "wlachischen" Wanderhirten der innerbalkanischen Berglandschaften aus. Auch ihre Führer nördlich der Donau tragen zu einem guten Teile kumanische Namen. Die Kumanen scheinen also an dieser grossen walachischen Nordwanderung einen beträchtlichen Anteil gehabt zu haben.

Um 1210 werden die Rumänen zum ersten Male sicher in Siebenbürgen erwähnt, und zwar in der Gegend von Fogarasch im südwestlichen Siebenbürgen. Dort hat sich um jene Zeit am Südhang der Karpaten unter der Schutzherrschaft des ungarischen Königs auch das älteste rumänische Staatswesen entwickelt. Wie die Namen zeigen, war die Herrenschicht wenigstens zu einem guten Teile turkvölkischer Abstammung. Die Haupstadt war zuerst Argesch, dann Campulung, schliesslich Targovischte. Im 14. Jahrhundert war dieser von Ungarn bisher abhängige Staat schon so erstarkt, dass sein Herrscher, der den türkischen Namen Basarab trug, es wagen konnte, die ungarische Oberherrschaft abzuschütteln. In dem Krieg, der darüber ausbrach, gelang es Basarab, das ungarische Heer in den Karpaten zu umzingeln und zu vernichten

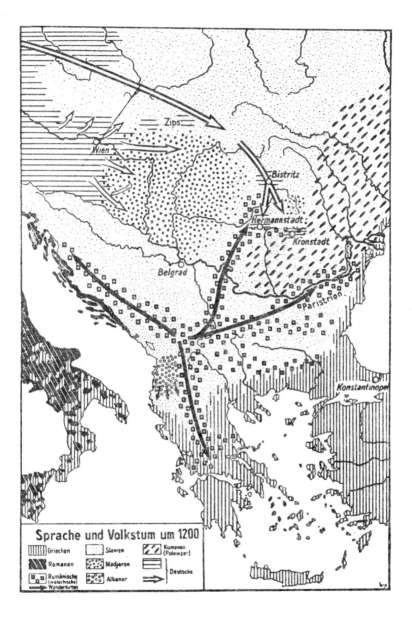

Sprache und Volkstum um 1200

Griechen	Slawen	Kumanen (Polowzer)
Romanen	Madjaren	
Rumänische (walachische) Wanderhirten	Albaner	Deutsche

Zips

Wien

Bistritz

Hermannstadt

Kronstadt

Belgrad

Paristrion

Konstantinopel

(1330). Auch dem mächtigen ungarischen König Ludwig dem Grossen (1342 — 1382) gelang die Unterwerfung der Walachei nur auf kurze Zeit. Bald rissen sich die Walachen wiederum los. 1369 wurde ein ungarisches Heer in der Walachei vernichtet. Damit war die Selbständigkeit des rumänischen Fürstentums der Walachei gesichert.

Im 14. Jahrhundert entstand das zweite rumänische Staatswesen. Um 1360 gründete der ungarische König eine Grenzmark Moldau, die rumänischen Woiwoden zur Bewachung gegen die von Osten drohenden Tataren anvertraut wurde. Ausgangspunkt dieser Staatsbildung war die Berglandschaft von Marmarosch (Maramuresch). Aber schon im Jahre 1365 riss sich dieses Vasallenfürstentum vom ungarischen Staate los und machte sich zum selbständigen Staate, dessen Schwergewicht sich nunmehr ostwärts an die grosse Handelsstrasse Lemberg — Suceava — Akkerman verlegte. Unter ständigen Kämpfen mit den Polen und Tataren wurde das Staatsgebiet, dessen älteste Hauptstadt das kirchen- und klosterreiche Suceava war, nach Norden und Osten ausgedehnt. — Die weitere machtpolitische Entfaltung der beiden rumänischen Fürstentümer wurde sehr dadurch gehemmt, dass im 15. Jahrhundert beide in ständige gegenseitige Kämpfe verwickelt waren.

*

Um die Achse des grossen Karpatenbogens hatte sich im 13. bis 15. Jahrhundert der mächtige rumänische Volkstumsblock herausgebildet. Aber die rumänische Siedlungsausbreitung beschränkte sich nicht auf das Gebiet beiderseits des Karpatenbogens — Siebenbürgen, Moldau, Walachei —, sondern sie erfasste von Siebenbürgen aus auch die Nachbarlandschaften Ostungarns. Dabei scheint diese Ausbreitung zunächst ausgegangen zu sein von drei Kerngebieten, die von den walachischen Wanderhirten zuerst besiedelt worden waren: Fogarasch, Marmarosch und Bihar. Diese drei Berglandschaften, deren Hochregion reich an ausgezeichneten Weideplätzen ist, scheinen die einwandernden Walachen besonders angelockt zu haben. Von dort aus wurde zunächst Siebenbürgen besiedelt, dann folgte die Ausbreitung von Siebenbürgen aus einerseits über die Karpaten nach der

Walachei und der Moldau hinüber, andererseits nach Nordwesten, dem Südhange der Karpaten entlang durch die Karpatenukraine und die Slowakei bis nach Mähren und bis an die Grenze Oberschleisens. In Mähren erinnert an diese grosse walachische Siedlungsbewegung noch heute die Landschaftsbezeichnung der "mährischen Walachei". Nachkommen walachischer Hirten sind wahrscheinlich auch die "Góralen", ein an der schlesisch-kleinpolnischen Grenze in der Hochregion der Karpaten sitzender Volkssplitter, der heute polnisch spricht, aber auf Grund anthropologischer und volkskundlicher Tatsachen auf die Walachen zurückgeführt werden muss. In den älteren Quellen werden die Góralen auch noch als *Valachi* bezeichnet. Die walachische Wanderungsbewegung hat weiterhin den grössten Teil Galiziens erfasst und darüber hinaus sind einzelne walachische Hirtenschwärme quer durch die Ukraine sogar bis nach Nordkaukasien vorgedrungen.

Diese "walachische" Ausbreitung als geschichtliche Gesamterscheinung darf freilich nicht restlos mit der Ausbreitung des rumänischen Volkstums gleichgesetzt werden. Der Name "Walache" bezeichnete damals nicht nur denjenigen, der rumänisch sprach, sondern einen jeden, der dieselbe soziale Lebensform wie die rumänische Hirtenbevölkerung hatte und der im Besitze des "walachischen Rechtes (*jus valachicum, jus valachale*) war. Dieses walachische Recht sicherte den Wanderhirten eine gewisse Vorrechtsstellung. Sie besassen unter ihren Woiwoden und Knesen eigene Verwaltung und eigene Rechtsprechung. Sie hatten nur geringe Abgaben zu entrichten und unterstanden unmittelbar der Finanzverwaltung der königlichen Kammer. Solche Vorrechte, die das ungarische Königtum den Walachen einräumte, übten eine ungeheure Anziehungskraft aus. Sie wirkten wie eine gewaltige Saugpumpe, durch die immer neue Schwärme walachischer Wanderhirten aus ihrer innerbalkanischen Heimat über die Donau herüber auf ungarischen Boden gezogen wurden. Hier konnte der apostolische König von Ungarn die walachischen Hirten zu Besiedlung der menschenleeren Grenzlandschaften gut gebrauchen. Den rumänischen Wanderhirten haben sich dann ukrainische und slowakische Gruppen angeschlossen. In den zeitgenössischen Quellen werden diese verschiedenen Gruppen nicht nach der Sprache unterschieden. Alle werden gleichmässig als "Walachen" bezeichnet. Die Nachbarstaaten — Böhmen-Mähren und Polen-Litauen — haben durch Übernahme des "walachischen Rechtes" die walachischen Hirtenschwärme auch auf ihr Staatsgebiet zu locken versucht, jedoch nicht mit demselben Erfolge wie Ungarn.

The Albanian-Rumanian Migrations
— 11th-13th centuries —

Summary

One of the major events changing the ethnic structure of Southeastern Europe in the 11th-13th centuries was the expansion of the Albanian-Rumanian settlement areas. Ca. 600 A.D., Avar-Slav tribes occupied most of the Balkan area. Parts of the Balkan Romanized population held out in the coastal areas somewhat longer. Another group of Romanized Balkan tribes, the ancestors of the Albanians and Rumanians, managed to survive as migratory shepherds in the mountanious regions, mainly in and aroud the northern part of Albania. After the Slavic invasion, for almost half a millenium, the Albanians and their relatives, the Rumanians (the Wallachians) had practically no real history. They only survived, not really participating in the historical events of the area. The Albanians appear in history in the 11th century — mainly as mercenaries. Later, they began to migrate and spread, mainly to the south and east, reaching even Italy. The Rumanians reappear in history in the 10th century when "Wallachians", still as migratory shepherds, are mentioned first time in the border area of Thessaly and Macedonia. In 972 A.D., the Byzantine Empire occupied the area known as *Paristrion*. Ca. 1100, the first small local dukedoms appear in the area of the present Dobruja, in which, apparently, the population was Rumanian, but the local chieftains had Cuman or Pecheneg names. The migration of the Rumanians into the area of the Carpathian mountains came, however, not from Dobruja, but from the migratory shepherds in the inner Balkan mountainous regions. It seems that also large number of Cumans participated in the northward movement of the Wallachians.

It was in 1210 that Rumanians are first mentioned in Transylvania, namely in the Fogaras district adjoining the northern slopes of the Southern-Carpathians. About the same time, south of Transylvania and the Carpathian mountains the very first Rumanian state-like unit developed under Hungarian protection. In the 14th century, another state-like unit arose in Moldavia, initially also under Hungarian rule, but it became independent in 1365. Thus, in the 13th and 14th centuries, around the axis of the Carpathian mountains, the Rumanian population spread, from which area they migrated in various direction, even reaching as far as present-day Slovakia. The "Wallachian" expansion, however, may not be seen as totally Rumanian. The name "Wallach" denoted not only those who spoke Rumanian, but also others who adopted the way of life of the Rumanian shepherd population and enjoyed special priviliges granted them by the Hungarian kings. These privileges which included the right for self-administration and jurisdiction under their own leaders, exercised tremendous attraction for Wallachian migratory shepherds who came in swarms from their Balkan homeland over the Danube into Hungarian land in Transylvania. The Hungarian kings had good use for the incoming Wallachians in resettling them in the unpopulated borderlands of the country.

A HUNGARIAN-RUMANIAN DIALOGUE

These are excerpts from a press review article, entitled "At the Danube," published in *The New Hungarian Quarterly* (Winter 1978).

In two consecutive Sunday issues, (Christmas 1977, and New Year 1978) the Budapest daily *Magyar Nemzet* printed a long article by the septuagenarian poet Gyula Illyés, entitled *Válasz Herdernek és Adynak* (A Reply to Herder and Ady).

His starting point is a statement by the Prussian preacher, poet and evolutionist philosopher Johann Gottfried Herder (1744-1803), who was among those who helped shape the young Goethe's mind. In his four-volume *Ideen zur Philosophie der Geschichte der Menschheit* ("Ideas toward a Philosophy of the History of Mankind"), first published in 1791, Herder, then a highly fashionable and widely read author, declared: "Of the Hungarians, small in number and wedged in between others, not even the language will be detectable as the centuries pass." The prognosis, Illyés points out, soon reached Hungarian intellectual circles. The effect, Illyés adds, did not, contrary to what most literary historians think, act as an incentive. It actually worsened the condition of a nation already seriously ill. After a century of ruthless Habsburg domination — in the wake of the 150-year Turkish occupation of the largest, central third of the country that had ended in 1686 — Herder's judgement came at a time, Illyés points out, when the leaders of an anti-Habsburg Jacobin conspiracy were being publicly beheaded in Buda in 1794. And it reverberated down the 19th century, seeming to justify and strengthen the feeling of doom expressed in marvellous poetry by the romantic poets Kölcsey, Berzsenyi and Vörösmarty. And again, after the failure of another, but this time large-scale anti-Habsburg uprising, the 1848-49 revolution and war of independance, when, in the wake of the 1867 Austro-Hungarian *Ausgleich*, despite all the economic boom it had produced, one-and-a-half million impoverished, desperate Hungarians emigrated to America.

He then goes on tracing the impact of Herder's prophecy a hundred years after it had been made. Endre Ady, one of the greatest poets Hungary has ever produced (1877-1919) felt he was "the last surviving Hungarian." Illyés explains why in detail. The Hungarian nation was doomed to extinction, Ady believed, unless a real revolution occured. He saw the catastrophic nature of the Great War long before it started and was fully aware of its inevitable consequences. He died in early 1919, fully vindicated by history, but what soon followed in terms of long-range suffering and deprivation on an unprecedented scale, redrawing the maps and cutting deep into the flesh of the nation, surpassed even his worst expectations. "For not even he had prophesied the kind of darkness that he saw approaching with his dying eyes," Illyés says. We have to realize this, otherwise "how could we perceive the light of hope of which we would like to talk at the end of these thoughts?"

Herder would not recognize the Hungarian nation today, Illyés goes on, standing once again on its feet after so many trials and tribulations. We have a firm social and economic order, our intellectual life also shows signs of healthy development, our situation may even seem enviable to many. But only two thirds of the fifteen million Hungarian-speaking people live within the frontiers of this country. That means that "one Hungarian in three, not knowing or, learning with great difficulty, the official langue completely alien to his own in its very structure, struggles with many and hitherto not sufficiently recognized difficulties. The basic reason for this being that in the face of the national irritability that sprang up in this century with such unexpected force, and chiefly of the impatience that is directed against national minorities, even the kind of humanism that socialism professes is ineffective."

There are no international agreements to protect the rights of national minorities, Illyés reminds us. "Peace Treaties, taking them for granted, relegate them among the human rights of the individual."

A Hungarian-speaking population exceeding a million (about 2.5 million — Ed.) and living in minority status has been deprived of its university where the language of tuition used to be its own. No other institutions of higher education in the language exist there any longer and soon there will be no secondary schools teaching in Hungarian either. As a consequence, young people will soon be unable to learn a trade in their own language. "In elementary schools small children are taught in their own language that their ancestors were barbarian invaders, inferior devastators . . . architectural masterpieces built by their ancestors are described as proof of their guilt." More than twenty percent of the children of the largest national minority in Europe are not even taught the alphabet in their own language. It often occurs that doctor and patient, who speak the same language, are compelled to communicate through an interpreter, thereby reducing the standards of medical service to a "jungle level." Young professionals, who want to retain their language, are often forced to take jobs far from their language territory, while alien-speaking individuals are posted among Hungarian-speakers. Ministers are not allowed to preach to the faithful in Hungarian.

"A national minority or another — just like nations — will lose the race nowadays by falling behind in the number of offspring it produces. That is, if the individual fails to receive from the community of his people the feeling of assurance that he will get protection for his offspring: a kind of community for which each can make a sacrifice and with no worries: with faith in the future."

Under the title "Huns in Paris," *Luceafărul,* the weekly of the Rumanian Writers' Association, printed an article by Mihnea Gheorghiu, a writer, Chairman of the Editorial Board of the paper, in its May 6th 1978 issue.

After summarizing briefly Illyés's introductory remarks as "a bizarre mixture of Hegelian dialectics and the echoing of Herder supplemented with some local lyrical motifs," the Hungarian poet, according to Gheorghiu, goes on "to construct a whole scaffold out of expiations based on totally subjective and imagined facts." Illyés reaches the conclusion, Gheorghiu says, that the treatment of national minorities in Rumania amounts to apartheid on a South African scale and, if not to ethnocide, then to definite ethnic oppression."

He adds that, on the occasion of the American visit of the Rumanian President, even Barbara Walters, the TV commentator, was told that "it would be highly desirable if the national minorities of the world would enjoy at least as many rights as the national minorities of Rumania do."

Not satisfied by this, Gheorghiu says, Illyés then declared as reported in a Reuter dispatch from Budapest that he was willing to take full responsibility for exposing the conditions of the Hungarian minority in Rumania.

Gheorghiu draws the conclusion that there must be something or someone "interested in heating up the gunpowderkeg again, and in putting the bourgeoist-nationalist apple of discord back into the basket of timeliness." Certain vile interests direct some people to fan "the cooling embers of ethnic rivalry" and "enemies of the working class" revive the slogans of revanchist nationalism and chauvinism.

In *Élet és Irodalom,* a Budapest literary weekly, for July 8th 1978, Zsigmond Pál Pach, the historian, head of the Institute of History of the Hungarian Academy of Sciences, and Vice-President of the Academy, tells of a conference of social scientists from the socialist countries held in Budapest in April 1978. The Academy of Social and Political Sciences of the Socialist Republic of Rumania had sent a large delegation, and Professor Pach gained the impression that they shared his views on the character of the conference, and the type of discussion needed. His surprise was therefore all the greater when he read an article in Luceafărul — the weekly of the Rumanian Writers' Association — "Huns in Paris" by Mihnea Gheorghiu.

Mihnea Gheorghiu "includes Gyula Illyés amongst those who 'regret that the lording of the lordlings came to an end with the victorious new social order;' as one who 'as the enemy of the working class reaches a stage where he evokes the blood and hatred provoking slogans of revanchist nationalism and chauvinism;' who supports the fascist gospel of *vivere pericolosamente,* 'full of nostalgia for a dualism whose sun has set and the memory of the admiral without a fleet,' feeling a 'gut-hatred' for members of other nations; doing all that in the 'hope that the wheel of history might turn back, perhaps to the wheel on which Horia* was broken.' I will not go on quoting similar, perhaps even rougher, unspeakable abuse.

Can one insinuate that this Hungarian writer is full of nostalgia for the Dualist and the Horthy age, for the memory of the admiral without a fleet? — asks Pach. A Hungarian writer who calls on the 1514 Dózsa peasant rebellion, jointly honoured by Hungarians and Rumanians, and the 'blood thirsty laws' of the noble national assembly that followed its suppression to bear witness in his work, amongst them those laws which 'over and above seizing every one of their human and even animal rights even keenly prescribes how they must be executed in any given case'? After all Gyula Illyés had fled West to Vienna, crossing the frontier illegally, in 1920, after the suppression of the 1919 Republic of Councils of Hungary, going on to Berlin, and later to France. There he not only met the most outstanding representatives of modern French intellectual and artistic trends, cooperating with them, but as a revolutionary poet he so to speak as a matter of course, participated in the socialist labour movement.

Like most of the great Hungarian poets Gyula Illyés as well has been thrilled by world literature and that of the neighbouring countries, an attitude that has never flagged. This is not a mere artistic test in his case either, but a conscious endeavour to familiarize others with the values of other national cultures, and to further the coming closer to each other and the friendship of the nations. Illyés has done much to interpret Rumanian literature as well. He transmitted not only the ballad 'Miorita' (Lambkin) to his Hungarian readers, but he turned another masterpiece of Rumanian balladry into a shared treasure of Hungarian literature. One could go on with George Cosbuc's famous "In the mountains" and Tudor Arghezi's "Testament" and "Secret psalm," these pearls of Rumanian literature which thanks to Illyés sparkle in the Hungarian in a manner worthy of the original. This then is the 'lair' which according to the author of the *Luceafărul* article gave a home to Illyés's 'nightmarish hostility to Rumanians?"

---

*Horia (b. 1730) led a Rumanian peasant rebellion in Western Transylvania in 1784 and was broken at a wheel in 1785.

"What I am inclined to say rather here is the recognition that one must make a final and radical break with every kind of pretty and poisoned thinking and nationalist discrimination. Hungarians, Rumanians, Slovaks, Germans, Ukrainians, Serbs, and Croats must and can only live like this here 'At the Danube' in these regions of East Central Europe that drag such a heavy historical burden."

Pach goes on to point out how opposed nationalisms grappled with each other in the Danube area between the Wars. As regards the relationship between Hungarians and Rumanians "a trend of political journalism became dominant, calling the tune on both sides, polluting and poisoning public opinion, presenting its own demands and grievances as absolute rights, and those of the other side as absolutely without justification . . ."

"And what was the result? Both countries turned defenceless against the Third Reich, becoming part of its *Lebensraum* and the satellites of German fascism. Hitler knew how to exploit the opposition between Hungarian and Rumanian nationalism. Northern Transylvania was "awarded" to Horthy, and Antonescu was helped to power in Rumania. They were used to keep each other in check, . . ." "Communists and progressives, Hungarians, Rumanians, and members of other nations, suffered together whatever side of the frontiers of the time they lived on. They sat next to each other in the dock, facing the judgement seat of state-power, be it Hungarian or Rumanian."

"Even as hunted game they fought together against every form of fascism, for social progress and national liberation. Those who tried to renew the traditions of Hungarian and Rumanian peasants who had fought together, of the true patriots who had attempted real unity in 1848/49, . . . were the pioneers who sowed the seeds of fraternal friendship between the two countries."

As Professor Pach points out however the realisation of this is not easy "as we thought", and even when the forties turned into the fifties. We fed on confidence at the time, and imagined, that the socialist transformation in itself would, as it were automatically, solve the national problem in the Danube region."

"We see things more realistically today. The minefields thrown by the centuries cannot be cleared in one sweep. National problems accumulated over a long period cannot be made to disappear from one day to the next. One cannot ignore them, or their remnants, perhaps applying temporary innovations, merely by referring to the friendship between the two nations."

As far as Hungarians are concerned, Professor Pach concludes, "we want to do all we can in the interests of cooperation between our nations. We are conscious of the fact that the internationalist road of strengthening confidence and friendship between the countries and nations of the Danube region is the only one that leads to the future."

ETHNOCIDE IN RUMANIA

By

MICHAEL SOZAN

The Transylvanian Hungarians, this over two million strong minority is suffering under the heavy-handed ethnic policy of the Socialist Republic of Rumania. Recent arrivals of refugees in the West uniformly tell of the horrors of ethnocide. Their case, I feel, should be brought to the notice of a growing number of Rumanianists outside of Rumania.

As far as I can tell, Western publications dealing with Rumania have been quite tolerant and accepting of the government's policies. Recent Rumanian versions of their history and ethnic origins have been written by politically motivated writers and are blatantly biased to the point of falsifying and inventing historical events. These works have not been looked at critically by Western scientists; in fact, they are rapidly being incorporated into recent publications as truly trustworthy material. I shall group my findings under five different topics. [*]

1. Ethnocide in Rumania

Let me give an operational definition of ethnocide. Any action by representatives of a dominant culture which aims at obliterating another sociocultural tradition through a coercive policy of assimilation is *ipso facto* ethnocide. Whatever the means, if any ethnic group loses its identity against its will, then we may talk about ethnocide. (For further clarification, see Jaulin 1970) Rumania employs two forms of ethnocide against its minorities: violent and non-violent. The uniqueness of ethnocide against Hungarians is its magnitude. Symptoms of minority dissatisfaction in Rumania include out-migration,

---

[*] A more complete list of biased publications (than in the present bibliography) can be found in an earlier version of this paper which appeared in *Current Anthropology*, March, 1979, Vol. 20. 1:135-148.

formal (constitutional) grievances, public disclosures by Rumanian citizens and by the international press, observations regarding the changing socioeconomic status of minorities, and demographic stagnation.

During and after the Hungarian revolution of 1956, the Rumanians government feared that Hungarians in Rumania would engage in a similar radical movement. The government allowed the detention of four revolutionary leaders (among them Prime Minister Imre Nagy) on Rumanian soil and carried out mass arrests. A document smuggled out of Rumania (see *The Observer,* April 14 and May 5, 1963) indicated "wide-scale arrests, deportation, and in some cases even executions of Hungarians" (Schöpflin 1966:133). The *Congressional Record* (August 8, 1964) revealed that close to 40,000 Hungarians were arrested, and in 1958 alone 56 of them were tried, of whom 10 were executed. Bailey (1964:26) reported that "thousands of Hungarians were arrested, perhaps hundreds put to death. In one trial alone in Cluj, thirteen out of fifty-seven accused were executed."

More recently, according to the Committee for Human Rights in Rumania (1977), in April 1977,

> as a part of a sweeping effort to silence all possible signs of independent-minded expressions within the Hungarian minority, the Rumanian secret police arrested scores of Hungarian intellectuals [who] were largely unknown to one another . . . . [They were] subjected to savage beating and other forms of torture . . . . The following are eight persons whose names are known: Jenö Szikszai, teacher from Brasov, Mrs. Jenö Szikszai, Brasov, Sandor Kuti, teacher from Brasov, Zoltan (?) Zsuffa, teacher from Covasna, Istvan Kocsis, dentist from Sfintu Gheorghe, Jozsef Haszmann, teacher from Papaut, Pal Kallay, clerk from Covasna, Peter Erös, librarian from Sfintu Gheorghe . . . . Jenö Szikszai, completely ruined physically and psychologically by torture, was found in the attic of his home shortly after his release—dead by hanging.

Nonviolent persecution affects not just isolated individuals, but an entire minority group (Schöpflin 1966:133):

> There is little doubt that Bucharest is working for the total fragmentation and assimilation of the Hungarian minority. Recent reports from Transylvania indicate that an atmosphere of terror is strongly in evidence there . . . . [Rumania] is probably the only place now

94

under communist rule where one still finds such manifestations—once characteristic of the Stalins era—as fear of contact with foreigners. Pressure on Hungarians to "denationalize" themselves is intense and unremitting.

Among the complaints widely reported in the world press we find the testimonies of communists (hardly a source of "anticommunist agitation" or "ad hoc political bloc"). First, there is evidence presented by Károly Király, vice-president of the Hungarian Nationality Workers' Council, alternate member of the Rumanian Communist Party's Politburo until 1972, and Central Committee member until 1975. In his letter to another member of the Central Committee (translated for the *New York Times*: Király 1978) he wrote: "Anxiety and concern compel me to write you about the manner in which the nationality question has been handled in our country of late . . . ." Enumerating blatant violations of the constitution (i.e., school policies, minority language usage curtailment, the elimination of Hungarian officials from towns and cities with a large proportion of Hungarians), Király continues:

> It is clear from only this much that a multitude of factual realities violate the Constitution . . . . the tendency is to forcefully assimilate nationalities in Rumania . . . . for millions of citizens it destroys their confidence in socialist society . . . . I am writing to you with a deep sese of responsibility, as I am one of those Communists who is convinced of the truth of our ideals . . . . We nationalities—Hungarians, Germans, Serbs, Jews, Gypsies, and so on—feel a deep respect for the Rumanian people and wish to live in harmony with them.

Michael Dobbs, a reporter of the *Manchester Guardian,* quotes Király, by then in internal exile in Caransebes (*Washington Post,* March 2, 1978):

> Government action includes the deployment of armed patrols, house to house arrests and the harassment and interrogation of hundreds of Hungarians . . . . He named 16 prominent Romanians who have asked to be associated with the appeal. Among them are Ion Gheorghe Maurer, a former Prime Minister, and Janos Fazekas, a Deputy Prime Minister and member of the decision-making political executive committee of the Romanian Communist Party.

Eric Bourne adds the following (*Christian Science Monitor,* May 2, 1978):

Last week, three more protests became known. Their authors were: Hungarian-born Deputy Prime Minister Janos Fazekas, who listed minority grievances in a letter to the party. Transylvanian writer and candidate member of the party committee Andras Sütö, who protested restrictions on Hungarian-language education. Lajos Takacs, a former rector of the Cluj (Transylvanian) University, which had separate Romanian and Hungarian faculties until the mid-1950's when all were merged under mainly Romanian direction . . . Mr. Takacs itemized 18 areas in which, he said, laws on minority rights were not being observed.

2. Ethnic policy and the Rumanian Legal code

The Nationality Statue of February 6, 1945, protected nationalities but was discarded after the 1947 peace treaties of Paris. In their Section II (Political Clause, Article 3), these treaties guaranteed equal rights to the inhabitants of Rumania without regard to race, language, religion, or ethnicity (see *Bulletin of the International Commission of Jurists* 1963). As early as April 2, 1949, the United Kingdom and the United States filed a strong letter of protest with the Rumanian government for the violation of human rights.

The Land Reform of March 23, 1945, while not overtly antinational, acquired an anti-Hungarian edge with expressed itself in the confiscation of Hungarian agricultural lands. The vast majority of those affected were Hungarians who had fled southern Transylvania during the "Antonescu terror." Also affected were "relocated" groups, soldiers in the Rumanian army, disabled soldiers, persons under medical treatment, the elderly unable to cultivate their land, and persons, who, in possession of a valid passport, happened to be in Hungary after August 1944. Only in exceptional cases were the officers of the Land Reform Committee Hungarian. While thousands of Hungarian peasants lost their land, among Rumanians even aristocrats were able to keep it.

Further confiscations of Hungarian property occurred under the C.A.S.B.I. Ordinance ("Cassa pentru Administrarea si Supravegherea Bunurilor Inamice"). The Hungarian Folk Federation protested these acts on more than three occasions in 1945 alone.

96

The New Citizenship Law of March 30, 1945, denied social benefits to those who were not in Rumania on October 11, 1944 (during the height of the terror just mentioned). This law was aimed directly at Hungarians who at this time were outside of Rumania or had opted for citizenship in northern Transylvania (which belonged to Hungary). It was supplemented by an executive order (August 17, 1945) declaring noncitizens all those who had escaped during the evacuation of northern Transylvania with the Hungarian or German armies. This law affected 300,000-400,000 refugees. Another decree, the so-called Patrascanu Decree 645, allowed the return of real estate to all Rumanians who for any reason whatsoever had alienated their land since 1940.

The constitutions of 1948 and 1952 guaranteed equal rights to nationalities and free use of minority languages in education and in political administration. These laws were systematically violated.

In 1952 Rumania formed the so-called Magyar Autonomous Province, with a Hungarian population of 565,510. The proof that this province was concocted purely for propaganda purposes vis-a-vis the West is that it included only slightly over one-fourth of the Hungarians of Rumania and that it gave them no pilitical or administrative power. Even this was replaced in 1960 by the Mures Autonomous Province, with a loss of 15% of the Hungarian (but with an addition of 20% Rumanian) population. In 1968 even the Mures Province was abolished, and the Hungarian members of the Provisional Advisory Committee and Executive Committee were arrested (Illyés 1976:123).

The constitution of 1965 does not reveal the country's departure from the foreign political, economic, and military policies of the Warsaw Pact nations. The equality of nationalities is reasserted in Decrees 57/1968, 24/1971, and 468/1971. In Section 22 the use of minority languages is guaranteed in those villages, cities, and counties were there is a "mixed population." The law requires the appointment of officials conversant in minority languages. In practice, however, Rumanian officials use only Rumanian. Király (1978) complains that the "use of the native tongue is severely restricted at meetings of the party, the Young Communist

League, the trade unions, and the various workers' councils; indeed, the use of the native tongue is prohibited even at meetings of the Nationality Workers' Councils." The violation of law with regard to the proportionate representation of minorities is reflected in Király's following words:

> With regard to the question of personnel, the replacement of Hungarian officials (where there still are any) with Rumanians is being carried out with incredible persistence. This applies equally to the politico-administrative apparatus and to the various economic and industrial enterprises. I don't even wish to think of such cities as, for example, Nagyvarad, where there is not a single party secretary of Hungarian nationality.

Since Hungarian (as well as Rumanian) newspapers are heavily censured, complaints are seldom voiced in journals. Yet sometimes one does get a glimpse from them of conditions in Transylvania. The Hungarian journal *Korunk* (Cluj), which is seldom allowed even to touch on minority grievances, braves the following statement (1971/10/:1467-68): "Except for the counties of Hargita and Kovaszna, in general, public signs, advertisements, etc., appear in Rumanian only. The same language is used for public transportation, trade, and mail traffic," even in almost totally Hungarian communities.

To summarize the discrepancies between law and practice, I will again quote Király:

> It is clear . . . that a multitude of factual realities violate the Constitution, the founding charter of the party and the fundamental principles set down and provided for in party documents. What is occurring in practice is not in harmony with the principles in these documents—indeed it completely contradicts them—and has nothing in common with Marxist-Leninism, fundamental human rights, humanism, or ethnical behavior and human dignity . . . .

I will now turn to the economic plight of Hungarians in Rumania. I will limit my descriptions to the bare minimum.

Sweeping changes in socialist Rumania have had a profound effect on the ethnic minorities. Not only have Hungarian "economic elites . . . experienced a fall from relatively high status," but workers and peasants have been shortchanged by policies applied against them in the course in industrialization, collectivization, and urbanization. One aim of the government is to block the entry of ethnic groups into predominantly Hungarian urban areas as well as into industry (*Erdélyből jelentik* 1977:61-62; Schöpflin 1966:133-34). Hungarians cannot acquire residence permits in the largest Hungarian cities — Kolozsvár (Cluj), Nagyvárad (Oradea), Arad, or the capital city of Székelyföld, Marosvásárhely (Tirgu Mures). They are sent to either Rumanian or German cities. This is why Sampson (1976a:328) found an influx of Hungarians into Feldioara. While more than an adequate number of Hungarian specialists is found in the vicinity of Hungarian cities, the general practice is to bring Rumanian skill there and locate Hungarian manpower in the "Old Kingdom" (*Erdélyből jelentik* 1977:63). For example, when the Azomures Chemical Plant opened in Marosvásárhely, Rumanians constituted 90% of the factory's employees. Similar practices characterize the factories of Kézdivásárhely (Tirgul Secuiesc) and Sepsiszentgyörgy (Sfintu Gheorghe), where the managers and skilled laborers are also Rumanians.

Repressive measures against Hungarian agricultural cooperatives deserve mention here. A complaint of refugees I have met is that the Rumanian government "borrows" agricultural equipment from Hungarian cooperatives during the summer months. Combines, tractors, and cultivators are taken to Rumanian agricultural regions where they are badly needed. At the end of the agricultural season they are returned — in poor repair. Obviously, in these cooperatives traditional forms of husbandry will survive longer than elsewhere.

3. Language usage and education in Rumania

One measure of ethnic policy in a nation in which 13 out of 100 persons claim to be members of minorities is the amount of freedom afforded to them in the use of their mother tongue in public life and education. The curtailing of minority language usage in Rumania was heavily underscored during the debates held by the Nationality Workers' Council on April 4-5, 1974. Here, the Hungarian, German, Serbian, and Ukrainian delegates protested against the Rumanianization policy of the Communist party. They were especially concerned over the impact of the Educational Reform of 1973 (which had a catastrophic effect on native-language usage in schools) and the general level of intolerance for the use of these languages in public. Party Secretary Ceausescu's reply to the exasperated delegates was, "The task of the minorities is to acquire the Rumanian language . . . /and to/ fulfill the plans of the Party, not to deal with such problems /as education and language maintenance/" (Illyés 1976:149-49, quoting *Korunk* 1974/4/: 521-23, translation mine).

Hungarian achievements in the arts and sciences in Transylvania have a rich past. Protestant colleges played a prominent role in the history of European higher education from the 17th century on. These institutions today are victims of governmental policies. In the absence of Hungarian universities, Hungarians have turned to their traditional folk culture.

Ex-Congressman (now New York City Major) Edward Koch made the following observation for the *Congressional Record* (1977): "I am distressed . . . at reports that indicate that discrimination taints many aspects of life for the Hungarian speaking minority. Last year I was shown a copy of the Romanian laws that now require a minimum of 25 students for any grade school class to be conducted in Hungarian, while only two students are required to form a class taught in the Romanian language." Statements similar to Koch's are found in the letter of Király (1978) cited earlier and in newspaper articles by Michael Dobbs (*Washington Post* and *Manchester Guardian*, March 2, 1978) and Eric Bourne (*Christian Science Monitor*, May 2 and May 25, 1978). Official Rumanian statistics on the number of Hungarian schools are analyzed by Szaz (1977), Illyés (1976:189-222), and *Erdélyből jelentik* (1977:50-61). One of Szaz's observations (p. 494) is that

> between 1957 and 1961 the Hungarian network of schools was abolished basically because of the emphasis laid by the Ministry of Education upon the learning the state language and to "prevent" national "isolation". The Hungarian and Romanian schools of the communities were merged into one school, or at least Romanian sections were opened in the formerly purely Hungarian institutions. The directors of the new schoold were in most cases Romanians with a Hungarian vice principal or vice director.

There was not only lively, but also deadly serious, interest in Hungarian-language maintenance at the Hungarian Bólyai

University (Cluj) when it merged with the Rumanian Babes University in 1959. An unprecedented event in the history of academic institutions followed this forced integration (Schöpflin 1966:133):

> It appears that one of the pro-rectors of the Bolyai University, Laszlo Szabedi, his wife, and five other university professors committed suicide. The impact of seven suicides on such a small town as Cluj was devastating and may have been one of the factors promting Bucharest to carry out its policies more circumspectly.

The *Times* (London) correspondent Dessa Trevisan had this to say (January 24, 1978): "The institute for medicine was also shut recently. By a special resolution, a Romanian faculty had been set up at the Hungarian academy for theatrical art which in effect meant the 'liquidation of the last little island of education in the Hungarian tongue.'"

Of 186 Hungarian *licees* in 1947, there remained 76 in 1976. Rumanian *licees* increased in number from 217 tó 568 between 1948 and 1968 (Committee for Human Rights in Rumania 1977:59).

A few words will suffice on the problems of mass communication in Hungarian. Even though "there is a substantial effort in Romania to publish periodicals and books in Hungarian," the Rumanian post office is sluggish in delivering them (when it does so at all). It complains of being overloaded. Subscriptions to Hungarian-language publications are taken at unannounced and random hours, and only one or two hours a month. Hungarian periodicals and newspapers are heavily censored and have very small circulations. The officials complain of a "paper shortage" (for details, see Illyés 1976:297-314). The content of Hungarian mass media programs is uninteresting and heavily burdened with political propaganda. There have been many complaints about the time schedule of these programs as well.

4. Rumanian historiography

"Recent Rumanian versions of their history and ethnic origins have been written by politically motivated writers and are blatantly biased to the point of falsifying and inventing historical events". Since this claim has been voiced time and time again in the West and the East, I will first quote one of the best-known authorities in the United States, Fischer-Galati (1978): "The political requirements made mandatory not only the reinterpretation of Rumanian history but also the falsification of data." Since the communist takeover, "the essential task of Roumanian historiography had been to provide a 'scientific basis' for validating the varying claims advanced by leaders of the Roumanian communist movement in search of legitimacy."

Rumanian histography points to Transylvania as the place of origin of the Rumanian people. Only Rumanian insist on the Transylvanian origin, and they have been maintaining it for the past two centuries without a shred of archiological or reliable historical evidence. In recent Rumanian interpretations of their origin taught in schools (see *Istoria Romanei* 1975, Giurescu 1968, Constantinescu 1970, Constantinescu and Pascu 1971), it is claimed that the present-day Rumanians are the descendants of Roman legionaries and the native Dacians, who mingled during the Roman occupation of Transylvania (A.D. 105-271). (It might be mentioned in passing that the Roman legions were made up not of Italians but of Dalmatians, Greeks, Macedonians, Iberians, Egyptians, Jews, Syrians, North Africans, and others and that during the influx of settlers the population was also mixed (Eutropius *Brevarium historiae Romanae* 8. 6. 2, quoted by Illyés 1976:360). Furthermore, even these ethnically mixed legions were frequently reshuffled in Transylvania within the provinces of Dacia and Traiana.) After the withdrawal of the legions, the descendants of the Romans and Dacians allegedly withdrew into the mountains, where so far Rumanian historians have failed to find any trace of them (Constantinescu and Pascu 1975:35, 55, 113-14, 118, 259, 297). Roman and Byzantine sources rich in observations regarding the Lower Danube region are silent on the Daco-Rumanians.

Rumanian scientists ignore reports written in the 1070s by the Byzantine general Kekaumenos, which represent the earliest and most authentic data on the Vlachs, the ancestors of the Rumanians (Litavrin 1972). While Kekaumenos maintained that the Vlachs were the descendants of the Dacians and the Besses, he placed their origin where the Danube and Sava Rivers meet and not in Transylvania. That his geographic information rests on solid grounds is attested by the fact that the Roman government, after the abandonment of Dacia, transferred this name to the regions south of the Danube. The memory of the short-lived Dacia Traiana and its original location were forgotten by late antiquity. Kekaumenos clearly states that during the 11th century the Vlachs inhabited Edessa, Macedonia, and Hellas, that is, the Balkans, where their linguistic relatives have survived to the 20th century. His reports are incompatible with the aims of Rumanian historians. Rumanian linguists claim the Rumanian language to be a Latinized derivative of the Dacian language. Since all linguistic data on this language have disappeared (Constantinescu and Pascu 1975:313-20), this statement is illegitimate.

Two medieval chronicles mention a people present in the general area of Transylvania at the time the Magyars arrived in the 9th century. One of these is the 11th-century *Chronicle of Nestor* (*Povesti Vremennyi Let* 1950, Trautmann 1932), the other the 13th-century *Gesta Hungarorum* (1975). Both are vague on the location of a people called "Voloch" (*Nestor*) or "Blachi" (*Gesta*). Since Rumanian historians refer to these Vlachs as their ancestors, it may be noted that all pastorals in the Balkans and in the Carpathian Basin were called Vlachs until at least the 13th century. While the *Chronicle of Nestor* is ambiguous as to the location of the Magyar-Vlach encounter, the *Gesta's* author is merely projecting his contemporary situation back 400 years. If we were to believe him in other respects, Hungarians would be the descendants of the Huns and would have been present in the Carpathian Basin early as the 5th century (Illyés 1976:356).

Based on these two chronicles, the officially approved Rumanian historiography explains that the descendants of the Daco-Roman population survived to the present and that their indigenous status in Transylvania is a proven fact. For this reason Giurescu (a professor at the University of Bucharest) claims that "Transylvania is *par excellence* the land of the Dacians, the Romanian people's forefathers" (Giurescu 1968: 134). Having finished this altogether politically motivated book of myths, often amusing in its invention and inversion of historical facts and names, the native reader may be indifferent to the total omission of the 1,000-year-long role of Hungary in organizing the demographic, economic, political and cultural life of Transylvania. He may even question whether European maps made by geographers are telling the truth. While people outside of Rumania are fortunate to have a more balanced picture because of the accessibility of reliable scholarship, Hungarians and Saxons in Rumania, whose forefathers were the important political leaders of Transylvania, are denied knowledge of how their ancestors shaped their past.

In the opinion of serious scholars—both Rumanian and foreign—the Daco-Roman origin theory is merely wishful thinking. According to Dinic (1966:560),

> The history of these people down to the later middle ages is obscure, and its origins are the subject of much discussion . . . . Outside Rumania, however, the more probable view is generally held that the origin of the Romanian people is to be found south of the Danube, in the romanised population of the Balkan peninsula which, after the Slav settlement, took themselves to the mountains to become a race of herdsmen.

Another authoritative source, George and Tricart (1954:239, translation mine) reflects upon Rumanian origins as follows: "The origins of the Rumanian nation have until the present been more obscure. The aforementioned theory of *continuity*, making the Rumanians the descendants of the Romanized Dacians, has now been abandoned." Other refutations of the Daco-Roman origin theory are found in Dami (1967:267), Densusianu (1901), Hurmuzaki (1876, 1878), Philippide (1975:112), Rosetti (1968), Stadtmüller (1950:207-8; 1965: 90), Arató (1975), Asztalos (1934), Bartha (1977), *Gesta Hungarorum* (1975), Hóman (1921, 1923), and Kniezsa (1938).

It is common European understanding that Rumania's acquisition of Transylvania was based not on "historical rights" but on international agreements in the 20th century by alliances that defeated Hungary in 1918 and 1945. The treaties made in 1920 (Trianon) and in 1947 (Paris) stipulated full political and human rights for the minorities. The fact that they have not been treated according to these international agreements has, in some measure, resulted in tension between Rumania and the Federal Republic of Germany and between Rumania and Hungary. Since Hungary has no recourse to active intervention on behalf of more than 2,000,000 Hungarians in Rumania, Rumanian xenophobia over Transylvania seems groundless. Therefore one may question the rationale behind what Fischer-Galati (1978) has called the "invocation . . . of the lessons of Roumanian history . . . for legitimizing Roumanian nationalism."

5. Rumanian statistics

If anything characterizes Rumanian statistics, it is unreliability. Ethnic minorities are notoriously underenumerated. This is a curious situation, since the growth of an ethnic minority usually enhances the international reputation of a country. Rumanian demographic data on ethnic minorities rest on two criteria: "nationality" and "language usage," as declared by the citizen. Eyewitnesses tell me that the Rumanian census taker is usually a member of the major culture, empowered with modes of intimidation and underenumeration. He is also given a free hand in making arbitrary decisions for respondents who do not fully understand the meaning of the questionnaires. There is considerable advantage — for furthering careers, getting special favors, etc. — in declaring oneself Rumanian rather than a member of a minority, and people find it similarly beneficial to Rumanianize their names. It is a commonly accepted practice to record Greek Orthodox Hungarians as Rumanians.

The Rumanian demographer Satmarescu (who cannot be accused of harboring pro-Hungarian and irredentist sentiments) comments (1975:426) on the poor quality of published demographic data on Transylvania, the "tendency to overestimate the Rumanian section of the population," and the "frequency with which the basic territorial units for demographic tabulation have been modified," including the county of Brasov. He discusses the inadequacy of "nationality" and "language" as criteria for "an entirely accurate statement on the minorities" and asserts that, since all these difficulties apply particularly to the Hungarian population, "there is thus every likehood that their numbers were significantly underestimated in 1966" (p. 432). He continues: "It is also rather surprising that the increase in the number of people with Hungarian as their mother tongue over the intercensal period was significant." He goes on to mention the proportionately decreasing Hungarian urban population (p. 433): "Whether or not it is a deliberate policy to reduce the strength of the Hungarian minority in the urban areas of Transylvania, there is evidence of administrative measures, such as the discriminatory allocation of housing units, which make it more difficult for rural Hungarians to move into the large urban centers than (for) their Romanian counterparts."

Satmarescu argues (p. 536) that

assuming [that the Hungarian population of 1.7 million in 1910 had] increased over the period 1910-66 at *a*) the average rate observed in Transylvania, *b*) the average rate observed in Romania, *c*) the average rate observed in Hungary, and *d*) the average rate of natural increase observed in Hungary, and making allowances for emigration and reparations associated with the two world wars, suggests a minimum expected Hungarian population in 1966 of 2.0 million and a maximum of over 2.5 million.

In 1966 the official Rumanian statistics held the Hungarian population to be only 1,600,000. Satmarescu concludes with skepticism that in 50 years the Hungarians lost between 400,000 and 900,000 of their numbers. This "loss" is all the more curious, he notes (p. 439), since "in most plural societies for which adequate information is available it is the minority groups that have the highest fertility rates and hence highest rates of natural increase."

A few more recentent measures may be mentioned here:

a) Confiscation of pre-World War II documents and archival materials. Under Decree Law 206/1974, the government is confiscating all personal, village, and organizational documents and placing them out of reach of their owners. Cerfificates of birth, marriage, death, and land ownership, wills, maps of townships, individual records of donation and sale, etc., have been removed from the possession of Hungarians and other minorities. Anthropologists interested in the history of, say, land tenure, kinship, political organization, and religion among these minorities may be suprised to find that all the village notary can offer them is recent records of collectivization. This is especially regrettable in light of the fact that Transylvania is one of those rare places in Europe in which communal village landownership and shifting agricultural prevailed until the end of the 19th century.

Church documents have been removed from villages without receipts and in total disarray. *Neuer Züricher Zeitung,* quoted by the *New York Times* (May 7, 1976), reasons as follows: "The intent behind the nationalization of the ecclesiastical archives is to sever the religious communities from their historical roots. A church without a past (tradition) has no future, especially one which represents a religious and national minority. The first victim of these war-like designs against the religious and cultural minorities by the Rumanian regime was the Hungarian Reformed church."

b) Ethnically homogeneous Szekler towns are being "integrated" with Rumanian populations, even when neither social nor economic conditions warrant it. The sociopolitical and economic organization of the villages has changed drastically in the past 30 years, in each instance favoring Rumanians even where they are a tiny minority.

c) Economic, political, social, and educational discrimination against Hungarian and other minorities at the national level. For minorities living in Rumania the term equal opportunity (which is guaranteed by the Rumanian constitution) is meaningless.

d) Restriction of contact between Hungarians living in Rumania and those in Hungary by limiting an individual's travel between these countries to once every two years. In addition, Decree Law 225/1975 prohibits non-Rumanian citizens from staying with Rumanian citizens overnight. (Exceptions are children and parents.) Lack of facilities for accommodation in rural Rumania makes visiting by relatives practically impossible.

6. **Pressure on internationally known persons** (i.e., Olympic champion Nadia Comaneci) **to Romanize their names.**

These examples are by no means exhaustive. Public ostracism of those speaking Hungarian outside the home, the assigning of Hungarian technical and educational experts to non-Hungarian areas, and many other practices have contributed to a rising rate of suicide, alcoholism, and demographic stagnation among the Szeklers.

The data cited here demonstrate that through political, legal (as well as illegal), social, economic, and educational means the Rumanian government aims to destroy Transylvanian Hungarian culture. Its motivation is obscure, since neither in Rumania nor in Hungary do Hungarians have any revisionist claims to Transylvania. The Hungarians of Rumania wish to live peacefully in a land they have inhabited for a millennium.

NOTES

1 There are convincing signs that Saxons, Jews, and other minorities also suffer from the heavy-handed Rumanian ethnic policies. The fact that a substantial portion of German-Rumanians emigrated to the Federal Republic of Germany as soon as the two nations had concluded the Reunification of Families Act of 1966 seems to suggest that they were dissatisfied in Rumania. This idea is supported by McArthur (1976a:363) who writes: "To check the youth's 'Romanianization' (Saxon) parents promote 'Germanization' even if they do not really like that either. German identity is thus the last boundry separating Saxons from Romanians." One must inquire about the reasons for Saxon emigration, since in Germany "the family is lonely, displaced and yearns for the comfort of the relatives they have left behind. Rather than return to Romania or otherwise admit that the dream has not come true, they write back and say: it's wonderful here, please come." In view of these findings, is it not possible that Rumanian ethnic policies are partly to blame for Saxon emigration? McArthur does not explore this possibility. Similarly, it is not difficult to assess the reasons Jews have been leaving Rumania at a rate of 3,000-5,000 a year since the 1950s (Gilberg 1974:458, quoting "well-informed sources in Washington"). Does the author of this article analyze growing anti-Semitism and ethnic policies in Rumania as possible forces behind Jewish emigration? He does not. For an analysis of Rumanianization, see Burks (1966:107), whose diagnosis of the fate of Saxons and Jews in Rumania is summed up in these words: "No doubt the time will come when both minorities will have virtually disappeared."

2 Among my sources is the Committee for Human Rights in Rumania. Since Hungarians neither in Rumania nor in Hungary have any way of opposing Rumanian policies, a group of their compatriots, the CHRR, was established in the United States in 1976. While I am not a member of this nonaligned organization I am familiar with its purpose and activities. Like other human-rights groups, it monitors grievances and publicizes discriminatory policies. Its paid political advertisements consist of quotations from Rumanian government communications and articles written by named staff cor-

respondents of newspapers with worldwide circulation (e.g., the *Manchester Guardian*, *Le Monde*, the *Washington Post*, the *New York Times*, the *Christian Science Monitor*, the *Times* /London/, *Neue Züricher Zeitung*, the *International Herald Tribune*, and others).

3 The intent of various policies regarding confiscation of minority property is analyzed by Schöpflin's (1966:120): "The assessment of the position of a minority under communist rule is complicated by the problem of gauging the extent to which repression is directed particularly and with special force at the minority group . . . The problem can be compounded when the standard of living of a minority is higher than that of the majority, as in the case of the Hungarians in Transylvania; the fact that their lands are confiscated and assets nationalized is not primarily determined by their nationality, but the effect is nonetheless to weaken their position as a nationality group."

4 "Les origines de la nation roumaine sont demeurées jusqu'a présent plus obscures. La these dite de la *continuité*, faisant des Roumains les descendants des Daces romanisés, est actuellement abandonée."

REFERENCES CITED

Arató, Endre. 1975. *A feudális nemzetiségtől a polgári nemzetig*. Budapest: Akadémiai Kiadó.

Asztalos, Miklós. 1934. *A nemzetiségek története Magyarországon*. Budapest: Lantos Könyvkiadó Vállalat.

Bailey, George. 1964. Trouble over Transylvania. *The Reporter*, November 19, pp. 25-30.

Bartha, Antal. 1977. A dákóromán kontinuitás problémái. *Magyar Tudomány* 2:145-56.

Bátky, Zsigmond, István Győrffy, and Károly Viski. n.d. *A magyarság néprajza. Vol. I. A magyarság tárgyi néprajza*. Budapest: A Királyi Magyar Egyetemi Nyomda.

Bulletin of the International Commission of Jurists. 1963. The Hungarian minority problem in Rumania. No. 17 (December), p. 35.

Burks, R. V. 1966. "The Rumanian national deviation," in *Eastern Europe in transition*. Edited by Kurt London, pp. 93-113. Baltimore: Johns Hopkins Press.

— —. 1978. "Nationalism and the rise of ethnicity," in *Ethnicity and nationality in Southeastern Europe*. Edited by Sam Beck and John W. Cole. Antropologisch-Sociologisch Centrum, Universiteit van Amsterdam, Papers on Mediterranean and European Soceties. In press.

Committee for Human Rights in Rumania. 1977. Arrests, torture and killing: New wave of anti-Hungarian terror in Rumania. MS. New York.

Constantinescu, Miron. 1970. *Etudes d'histoire Transylvanie*. Bucharest.

Constantinescu, Miron and Stefan Pascu. Editors. 1971. *Unification of the Romanian state: The union of Transylvania with Old Romania*. Bucharest: Publishing House of the Academy of the Socialist Republic of Romania.

— —. Editors. 1975. *Relations between the autochthonous population and the migratory populations of the territory of Romania*. Bucuresti: Editura Academiei Republicii Socialiste Romania.

Dami, Aldo. 1967. *La controverse de la continuité daco-roumaine*. Humanitas, Ethnica, Ethnos 5. Wien-Stuttgart.

Densusianu, Ovid. 1901. *Histoire de la langue roumaine*. Paris.

Diamond, Stanley, Bob Scholte, and Eric Wolf. 1975. Anti-Kaplan: Defining the Marxist tradition. *American Anthropologist* 77:870-76.

Dinic, M. 1966. "The Balkans," *The Cambridge medieval history*, vol. 4, pp. 519-65.

Erdélyből jelentik. 1977. New York: American Transylvanian Federation.

Fischer-Galati, Stephan. 1967. *The new Rumania: From people's democracy to socialist republic.* Cambridge: M.I.T. Press.

— —. 1978. The continuation of nationalism in Romanian historiography. *Nationalities Papers.* In press.

George, Pierre, and Jean Tricart. 1954. *L'Europe centrale.* Vol. I. Paris: Presses Universitaires de France.

Gesta Hungarorum. 1975. Budapest: Magyar Helikon.

Gilberg, Trond. 1974. Ethnic minorities in Romania under socialism. *East European Quarterly* 7:435-58.

Giurescu, Constantin. 1968. *Transylvania in the history of the Romanian people.* Bucharest: Meridiane.

Hitchens, Keith. 1969. *The Rumanian national movement in Transylvania, 1780-1849.* Cambridge: Harvard University Press.

Hóman, Bálint. 1921. *A székelyek eredete.* Budapest: Magyar Nyelvtudományi Társaság.

— —. 1923. *A magyarok honfoglalása és elhelyezkedése.* A Magyar Nyelvtudományi Kézikönyve I (7).

Hurmuzaki, Eodoxiu. 1876. *Documente privitoare la istoria romanilor.* Bucuresti.

— —. 1878. *Fragmente zur Geschichte der Rumanen.* Bucuresti.

Illyés, Elemér. 1976. *Erdély változása: Mitosz és valóság.* München: Aurora.

Istoria Romanei: Manual pentru anul IV licee de cultura generala si de specialitate. 1975. Bucuresti.

Jaulin, Robert. 1970. *La paix blanc: Introduction a l'ethnocide.* Paris: Editions du Seuil.

Király, Károly. 1978. An ethnic Hungarian communist in Rumania complains to his party about bias. *New York Times,* Feb. 1.

Kniezsa, István. 1938. *Magyarország népei a XI. században.* Budapest.

Koch, Edward. 1977. Contemporary educational policies in Transylvania. *Congressional Record* 123:51.

Litavrin, G. G. 1972. *Soviety i rasskasy Kekavmena.* Moskva.

Macartney, C. A. 1937. *Hungary and her successors 1919-1977.* London, New York, and Toronto: Oxford University Press.

McArthur, Marilyn. 1976a. The Saxon Germans: Political fate of an ethnic identity. *Dialectical Anthropology* 1:349-64.

Philippide, A. 1975. *Istoria stiintelor in Romania: Lingvistica.* Edited by Iorgu Iordan. Bucuresti.

Povesti Vremennyi Let. 1950. Moscow-Leningrad.

Prodan, D. 1971. *Supplex Libellus Valachorum, or The political struggle of the Romanians in Transylvania during the 18th century.* Bucharest: Publishing House of the Academy of the Socialist Republic of Romania.

Rosetti, Alexandru. 1968. *Istoria limbii romane de la originipina in secolul al VII-lea.* Bucuresti.

Sampson, Steven. 1976: "The city comes to the peasant." *Dialectical Anthropology* 1:321-48.

Satmarescu, G. 1975. The changing demographic structure of the population of Transylvania. *East European Quarterly* 8:425-39.

Schöpflin, George. 1966. "National minorities under communism in Eastern Europe," in *Eastern Europe in transition.* Edited by Kurt London, pp. 117-41. Baltimore: Johns Hopkins Press.

Stadtmüller, George. 1950. *Geschichte Südosteuropas.* München: R. Oldenburg.

— —. 1965. *Grundfragen der europaischen Geschichte.* München and Wien: R. Oldenburg.

Szaz, Z. 1977. Contemporary educational policies in Transylvania. *East European Quarterly* 11:493-501.

OUR CONTRIBUTORS

ANDRE DU NAY is the pseudonym of a prominent European scholar of Romance Philology. The pseudonym is forced upon him by political circumstances in Rumania. His most recent work, *The Early History of the Rumanian Language*, appeared in 1977 as part of the Edward Sapir Monograph Series in Language, Culture and Cognition, published by Jupiter Press.

LÁSZLÓ RÉTHY (1851 – 1914) was a Hungarian numismatologist, archeologist, and director of the National Museum in Budapest. His study, *The nationalities of Dacia during the Roman Period*, was first published in 1886 in the Yearbook of the National Archeological and Anthropological Society in Budapest.

THOMAS SZENDREY was educated in Hungary, Austria, and the United States. He received his Ph.D. from St. John's University, New York. He is an associate professor of history at Gannon University, Erie, Pennsylvania.

JEAN CSONKA is professor at the Ecole Superieure de Commerce in Neuchatel, Switzerland. He studied in Budapest, Paris, and at the Institut Universitaire de Hautes Etudes Internationales in Geneva, where he received his Ph.D. in Law and History. His study, *La version la plus récente de la théorie de la continuité daco-roumaine*, was first published in the *Documentation sur l'Europe Centrale* (Documentation on Central Europe), a periodical issued by the Institute for Research of Central Europe (Louvain, Belgium, 1979).

GEORG STADTMÜLLER is Professor Emeritus of History, University of Münich. He was department chief, East European Institute, Breslau (1935), professor of history, University of Leipzig (1938) and University of Münich (1950). He was director of Osteuropa-Institut and editor *Jahrbücher für Geschichte Osteuropas* (1960-1975). Author: *Geschichte des Peloponnes* (1944); *Geschichte Südosteuropas* (1950), *Geschichte des Völkerrechts* (1951); *Rechtsidee und Machtpolitik in der amerikanischen Geschichte* (1957); *Geschichtliche Ostkunde* (1959); *Die neue sowjetische Weltgeschichte* (1960), *Geschichte Südosteuropas* (1976, second edition).

MICHAEL SOZAN is professor of anthropology, Slippery Rock State College, Pennsylvania. He received his Ph.D. in anthropology from Syracuse University. He published a monograph on *The history of Hungarian ethnography* (University Press of America, 1977) and is currently preparing a comparative monograph on two villages in Austria and Hungary.

ABOUT THE EDITORS

STEPHEN BORSODY is Professor Emeritus of History, Chatham College, Pittsburgh. He was a diplomat and journalist in Hungary. J. U. Dr., Charles University, Prague; Privatdocent in East European history, University of Budapest. Author: *The Triumph of Tryanny: The Nazi and Soviet Conquest of Central Europe* (London and New York, 1960); *The Tragedy of Central Europe* (New York, 1962; revised and updated edition, New Haven, 1980). Contributor: *The Development of Historiography*, ed. Matthew A. Fitzsimons et al. (Harrisburg, Pennsylvania, 1954); *Czechoslovakia Past and Present*, ed. Miloslav Rechcigl (The Hague, 1969); *The Austrian Empire: Abortive Federation?*, ed. Harold J. Gordon, Jr., and Nancy M. Gordon (Lexington, Massachusetts, 1974); *The Hungarian Revolution of 1956 in Retrospect*, ed. Béla K. Király and Paul Jonas (Boulder, Colorado, 1977).

NANDOR DREISZIGER received his graduate diploma in Russian and East European Studies, and his Ph.D. in History from the University of Toronto. He is teaching courses in European, Russian and Canadian history at the Royal Military College of Canada. Author: *Hungary's Way to World War II* (Toronto, 1968) and numerous articles in anthologies and periodicals including the *Journal of Modern History*, the *East European Quarterly*, and the *Canadian Historical Papers*. He has also edited three collections of essays, *The Hungarian Revolution Twenty Years After: Selected Papers and Perspectives* (Ottawa, 1976), *Hungarian Poetry and the English-Speaking World* (Ottawa, 1977). He is the founding editor of the *Canadian-American Review of Hungarian Studies*.

ADAM MAKKAI is Professor of Linguistics at the University of Illinois at Chicago Circle. He is the foundation Executive Director of LACUS, Inc., the Linguistic Association of Canada and the United States, and Editor-in-Chief of the Association's tri-quarterly, *Forum Linguisticum*. His Ph.D. in general linguistics is from Yale, his B.A. degree is from Harward. He came to the USA as a Hungarian refugee in 1956 from Budapest. His main area of research is in semantics and lexicography. Author: *Idiom Structure in English* (Mouton, The Hague, 1972); *A Dictionary of Space English* (Chicago, 1973); *A Dictionary of American Idioms* (Barron's Educational Series (Woodbury, N.Y., 1975).

GEORGE SCHÖPFLIN is Joint Lecturer in the Political Institutions of Eastern Europe at the London School of Economics and the School of Slavonic and East European Studies, University of London. He was formerly on the staff of the BBC External Services. He has published widely on contemporary East European affairs and is currently working on the problem of nationalism in the area. He is the author of *The Hungarians of Rumania* published in 1978 by the Minority Rights Group, London.

LOUIS L. LŐTE is president of the *Committee of Transylvania, Inc.* He completed his studies in Hungary and the United States. With M. Eugen Osterhaven he is co-editor of *Transylvania, the Pathos of a Reformation Tradition* (Holland, Michigan, U.S.A., 1968). He is founder and editor of the *Carpathian Observer*. Author of numerous articles on national minorities. He is also editor of the *Székely Nép*.